East Coast KETO

TIPS & LESSONS TO HELP SIMPLIFY YOUR KETOGENIC LIFESTYLE

Bobbi Pike

WITH SIDEKICK
Geoff Pike

BREAKWATER

P.O. BOX 2188, ST. JOHN'S, NL, CANADA, A1C 6E6
WWW.BREAKWATERBOOKS.COM

COPYRIGHT © 2019 Bobbi Pike
ISBN 978-1-55081-786-7

A CIP catalogue record for this book is available from Library and Archives Canada.

 We acknowledge the financial support of the Government of Canada and the Government of Newfoundland and Labrador through the Department of Tourism, Culture, Industry and Innovation for our publishing activities. PRINTED AND BOUND IN CANADA.

Breakwater Books is committed to choosing papers and materials for our books that help to protect our environment. To this end, this book is printed on a recycled paper and other controlled sources that are certified by the Forest Stewardship Council®.

• •

The information provided in *East Coast Keto* represents personal opinion and experience and does not replace professional medical or nutritional advice. Always consult your physician or a health-care professional before starting any nutrition or exercise program to determine if it is right for you.

Our journey as foodies (and more recently as ketonians) changed for the better when we met Chef Roary MacPherson.

Over the years, we have shared many a glass of cheer, dined on delectable meals, and have created lots of wonderful memories together. We have worked with him at culinary events, feasted together at family celebrations, and socialized at each other's homes. We have also been privileged enough to be invited to work in the kitchen alongside Roary and other talented Newfoundland chefs. Through Roary, we have been introduced to a multitude of local and visiting chefs that can only be described as culinary royalty.

Chef Roary himself has been living a very successful low-carb journey, and we are always excited to be able to share our keto creations with him.

Not only has Roary been a source of inspiration, he has also become a great friend, a mentor, a sounding board, a culinary coach, and has been the provider of many tips and tricks to help us in the kitchen.

We dedicate this book to our wonderful friends.
To "King of the Cod," Chef Roary MacPherson,
his lovely wife, Kathy, and super-cool kid, Luke.

It scares me to look back at the path I was travelling in my pre-keto days and the health issues that were a (growing) part of my life. I thank our amazing family doctor for giving me the tools that brought me great health gains and probably added years to my life. Thank you for having the answers I needed and for keeping me accountable for my health journey. I am forever grateful.

To the wonderful folks at Breakwater, for giving me the opportunity to scream it from the rooftops.

To my ever so "word smart" editor, Marianne Ward, for keeping me on the straight and narrow when my creative brain wanted to fly off into literary (and culinary) tangents. Even if she wouldn't accept the capital K for Ketonians (as in from the planet Keto). It was a pleasure working with you.

To my family and friends, for being my taste testers and guinea pigs during my many attempts to keto-fy family favourite recipes.

To Laurie, for being my advisor, my weekly sounding board and confidant.

To Barb, for helping me through the rough days and making me smile, even when you were too sick to do it. I miss you, XO.

To my frikkin amazing hubby and sidekick, Geoff; a huge thanks for putting up with me burning the midnight oil while I worked though late-night writing sessions, for keeping me smiling in the kitchen and out, and for holding my hand through this keto journey. I see you... You are truly my "bess fren."

Bobbi Pike
Topsail, Conception Bay South, NL
June 2019

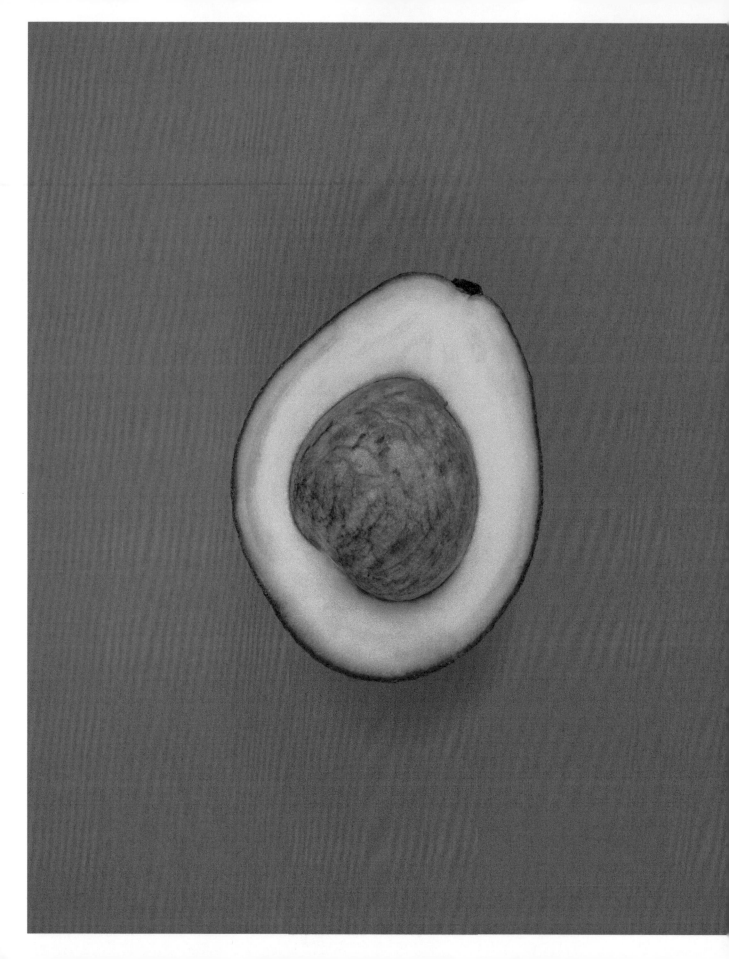

CONTENTS

Introduction | 9

Introduction

You could say the meeting of the minds that would become the *East Coast Keto* couple was a long time coming. Geoff was the boy next door. We went to the same school, played on the same grassy fields, then grew up and went our separate ways. We reconnected late in life, after both going through failed attempts at starter marriages. Even though I swore I would never marry again, I was defenceless to this guy. It just felt right. We walked across a Jamaican beach together on May 5, 2010, and said, "I do."

Then we settled into happily ever after. Among all the things that clicked in our new life together was our mutual love of cooking. Many couples bicker in the kitchen, but our kitchen dance was almost hypnotic. We finished each other's sentences and were interchangeable in life and also in the kitchen. We contentedly worked side by side as we lived, loved, and cooked, merging our "good" individual dishes into expressions of love and culinary delight. One of us would start a dish and the other would seamlessly move in and add our own tweaks. Our final dishes were a joint effort, creations of our love of life and all its flavours. We were happy.

As time passed, our love grew. Unfortunately, our girth grew along with the passion in our hearts. Year after year, our waistlines expanded to the point where the shadows our bodies cast as we held hands were unrecognizable to us both. We began to worry about our health, so we dug in and started researching.

I had heard the theories of "low carb" and "keto" being tossed around by a handful of people who had unsuccessfully gone through several "pay-to-play" weight-loss programs. They had all lost weight, but after they stopped paying weekly, they found they gained it back again. It wasn't sustainable in real life. Not to mention that health shouldn't come at the cost of weekly fees, meetings, and weigh-ins. Something was missing from these programs. I watched from afar. I requested membership to several low-carb and keto groups. I listened and learned.

Our first steps in this new world took us down the low-carbohydrate highway. We cut all white carbs from our lives: breads, pastas, grains, and potatoes. It was a slow and calculated process. We realized that it had taken us a while to gain the weight, so if we wanted to successfully lose it and still be healthy, losing should be gradual too. We noticed a difference right away—less bloat, some weight loss, a general feeling of "something good is happening here."

In the meantime, I kept researching and reading. In my uneducated state, I guffawed at so many of the posts that came across my social-media feed. These people had to be out of their minds doing this "ketogenic thing" to their bodies. It couldn't really be good for you. Right?

The next step in our progress toward sustainable weight loss had us discussing keto and low carb with our doctor. I fully expected her to tell us that keto wasn't a healthy choice, that it was just another fad. I can still remember sitting in our doctor's office, gobsmacked, listening to her tell us that, if done correctly, keto was a very healthy way of life. She went on to explain how the sugar industry had been lying over the years, that much of what we had learned about nutrition was wrong. Despite what we had been led to believe, eating dietary fat was in fact good for us.

In our grandparents' time, eating habits were very different. They lived off the land and raised livestock to feed their families. They consumed healthy animal fats and the vegetables that grew in their own garden. There was no mystery as to the ingredients they ate because they grew it all themselves.

Things drastically changed a little over sixty years ago when the sugar industry launched an advertising campaign to sell more product, arguing that sugar was good for us while consuming dietary fat was bad. You can read more about this in our article "Sweet Little Lies" at eastcoastketo.com.

With our doctor's approval ringing in our ears, we decided to give keto a go. We realized that the low-carb steps we had taken were just the tip of the iceberg and that we still had much to learn. Our research led us down a rabbit hole of information that was more than confusing. Each article we read contradicted the last—everybody had a different idea of "how to keto," and they were all trying to shout louder than the next guy.

We eventually found our way through all that conflicting information and stepped back from many of the social-media groups. We had chosen a drama-free life path and an uncomplicated lifestyle. We wanted the same for our keto life.

From this, the concept of *East Coast Keto* was born. We wanted to share our version of how to successfully keto without drama and stress. We wanted to help our friends discover that they could keto on their own without paying to weigh in every week. We wanted to share our information and encourage others to research for themselves. We wanted to share our love of food. Our knowledge learned from building our *Bobbi Pike Art* website meant we already had the tools for creating a keto website, and we already had all our favourite recipes that we had been busy keto-fying. We had all our newly acquired knowledge and a solid backing of life experiences to round it out.

So here we are! While Geoff likes to say we've lost a whole person between us, it's really not about how much weight we have lost—our journey has been so much more than that. Between us, we have reduced inflammation, stopped migraines, reversed diabetes, and cured acid reflux and chronic heartburn. The pre-keto blood pressure meds have been gradually lowered (with help from our Doc), and our blood pressure and our health in general is great! Our friends tell us we look twenty years younger than our pre-keto selves, almost as if we have found the fountain of youth!

We continue to shrink. We continue to keto. We continue to be happy. We welcome you to join us as we figure out the next steps in our journey.

ketosis:

the state the body enters when
there is no supply of carbohydrates for
energy; also occurs during times of no
food intake. Babies are born into ketosis;
it is our default metabolic state.

ketogenesis:

the production of ketone bodies
as the body breaks down fatty acids

ketone:

the chemical produced when
glucose is not available, typically through
restriction of carbs, and the body breaks
down fats for energy;
alternate fuel for your body

keto:

a short-hand term for the adjective
ketogenic (also used as a verb)

ketonian:

someone who has fully adopted
the keto way of eating

Keto 101

THE ORIGINS OF KETO

Most ketonians are under the impression that keto got its start back in the 1920s, but the ketogenic diet originated in the 1800s. William Banting, a wealthy Londoner, realized in his sixties that his health was not what it should be. He consulted with a Dr. William Harvey who directed him to change his diet because the traditional diet of most Londoners was too "starchy and sweet." Banting produced a booklet called *Letter on Corpulence* in which he described his experience with this new diet and how it made him feel. While Banting's diet was not quite as low-carb as the current ketogenic diet, it is the predecessor of what we now know as keto.

The first sign of keto in North America was in the 1920s when doctors at the Mayo Clinic used the ketogenic diet as a tool to control convulsions in people with epilepsy. They noticed that patients had fewer symptoms when they had lower blood sugars. They cut the supply of carbohydrates and allowed the body to burn fat for energy.

Although the use of a ketogenic diet as treatment for epilepsy was eventually replaced by anti-convulsive drugs, it seems things have come full circle, as keto is currently listed on epilepsy.com as a suggested treatment.

KETO IN A NUTSHELL

The basic concept of keto is to reduce carb intake in order to force the body to burn fats as energy. In today's typical Western diet, the human body has been trained to get its energy from carbohydrates (sugar and starches), which produce glucose in the digestive process. In a ketogenic diet, the body learns to burn fat as fuel instead of the glucose produced by carbohydrates.

We grew up thinking of our digestive system as a one-compartment system. We eat food, it goes into our stomach where it's processed, and then waste is expelled from our body. In reality, we should think of our digestive system as a two-compartment system. Think of the two compartments as a fridge and freezer.

In this scenario, our fridge is full of carbs and the back-up system is our freezer, which is full of fats. In a Western diet, our fridge is always chockablock with carbohydrates, so our body, like a hungry teenager, reaches into the fridge for fuel and quickly finds what it needs: a quick fix that is not nutritious. As often as the fridge is emptied, we quickly reload it with more carbs, and because that supply is never depleted, we never have to open the door to the freezer. The fats in the freezer not only stay intact, but also keep increasing as the excess carbohydrates located in the fridge turn into more fats, which overflow out of the fridge (and in turn cause accumulation on our waistline).

When we decide to forego carbs, an interesting thing happens. The body first goes to the fridge for energy. When it realizes the fridge is now empty, it doesn't skip a beat—it automatically reroutes and heads to that overfull freezer. It opens the padlock and swings the door open and finds its new source of fuel. As long as we keep that fridge empty (in the case of a ketogenic diet, below 20 grams of carbs daily), the door to the freezer remains open. Overnight, our body changes from a sluggish system that kicks into high gear to a highly efficient, fat-burning machine.

The secret to curing overeating is by curing hunger. We cure hunger by eating healthy fats. Healthy fats not only cure (i.e., satisfy) our hunger, they provide us with a stable source of energy.

WHY SHOULD WE CUT CARBS?

To learn about carbohydrates, we have to step into the world of nutrition. The food we eat does a lot more than fill our tummies—it provides us with the nutrients we need to grow, repair ourselves, and survive as a system. Food contains micronutrients and macronutrients. The micros are our vitamins and minerals. The three main macros are fat, protein, and carbohydrates. Each has a different purpose.

Fat aids vitamin absorption and hormone production, provides a source of energy, and helps us feel full and satisfied. Fat provides our bodies with fatty acids, two of which—omega-3 (alpha-linoleic acid) and omega-6 (linoleic acid)—are essential.

Omega-3 can be found in fish oils, leafy green veggies, flax seed, hemp, and walnuts. Omega-6 is known to fight infection, helps regulate the immune system, and helps with blood pressure levels and blood clotting. While both of these fatty acids are essential, sometimes there can be too much of a good thing. Research shows that finding the correct ratio of both is important. Too much omega-6 can cause your body to retain water, cause major inflammation, and raise blood pressure.

Protein gives us amino acids, which provide structure and support for our enzymes, muscles, organs, bones, and hair, and also help support a healthy immune system.

KETO FOOD PYRAMID

Carbohydrates are made up of carbon, hydrogen, and oxygen. They provide a cheap burning fuel for our bodies. The three types of carbs are sugar, starch, and fibre. There are no essential carbohydrates.

Starches and sugars break down into glucose, which is the simplest form of carbohydrate. The glucose then enters the bloodstream, causing blood-sugar levels to rise. This rise in blood sugar triggers the pancreas to produce the hormone insulin. Insulin then tells the cells to absorb the glucose and convert it for energy or store it as body fat. The insulin goes to work using up all the sugars, causing a sugar low. This often leaves us with cravings and feelings of hunger, causing us to consume more food, particularly carbs.

Many people get to adulthood before they realize that carbs turn to glucose in our body. Some never learn it at all. Cutting carbs from our diet is the simplest method of becoming a ketonian.

QUALITY MATTERS IN CARBS

Whole carbs are found in unprocessed foods that contain natural fibre, such as vegetables, whole fruit, and legumes. While fibre itself doesn't provide energy, it does feed the friendly gut bacteria, which cause the fibre to produce fatty acids that can be used as energy.

> We all know the gastrointestinal tract, or gut, has an important job within the body. Our gut hosts over 40 million bacteria that keep our bodies and brains functioning as they should. These bacteria not only affect digestion but also help to regulate immunity, emotional stress, and chronic illnesses, including cancer and type-2 diabetes.

KETO-FRIENDLY FOODS THAT HELP PROMOTE A HEALTHY GUT:
Avocado, berries, butter, coconut oil, fermented foods (such as sauerkraut and kimchi), kefir, nuts and seeds, and sour pickles.

Studies show that consuming an abundance of carbs, especially refined carbohydrates, can lead to insulin resistance and can be associated with health problems like obesity and type-2 diabetes. Refined carbs typically found in the Western diet are known to cause insulin dips and spikes, and that's not a good thing. Healthy eating is associated with keeping your insulin level at an even, low rate all day.

There is no such thing as an essential carb.

The standard, most widely accepted version of keto is low carbs, moderate protein, and high fat—5 percent, 25 percent, and 70 percent of your daily diet respectively. Don't worry about calories; that's part of the old way of thinking. Your main consideration is to make sure your carb intake is low, about 20 grams daily.

Insulin resistance is when cells start ignoring the signal that insulin is trying to send out—leading to high blood-sugar levels.

When the body becomes resistant to insulin, it tries to cope by producing even more insulin. People with insulin resistance are often producing much more insulin than healthy people.

Keto isn't about counting calories—it's about counting and cutting carbs and chemicals.

DO YOUR RESEARCH

So you want to get started and you're not sure where to start. The trouble is, every keto webpage brings up conflicting information, and the more you read, the more it confuses you.

Everybody seems to be talking about the ketogenic lifestyle these days: sports jocks, celebrities, and media, all speaking out about the pros and cons of ketosis, and it comes with a lot of bad information skewed by personal opinion. Let's try and cut through some of the malarkey and figure out what's real and what's not.

MYTH 1: KETO IS FOR WEIGHT LOSS ONLY.
While many talk about the weight-loss possibilities of ketogenic living, there is so much more to keto. Researchers are studying ketogenic living as a tool to possibly prevent or lessen the effects of Parkinson's, Alzheimer's, cancer, diabetes, autism, and epilepsy.

Ketosis has been shown to reduce blood sugars, lower blood pressure, lessen symptoms of polycystic ovary syndrome, decrease and lessen severity of migraines, and drastically reduce toxic inflammation.

Research on the anti-inflammatory effects of a keto diet is very intriguing. Over time, chronic inflammation can erode tissue, potentially damaging arteries and organs and contributing to diseases such as Alzheimer's and cardiovascular disease. The keto diet is anti-inflammatory both due to the foods it eliminates and those foods it includes. High-fibre carbohydrates like leafy greens, cauliflower, and Brussels sprouts, and healthy fats and oils—including anti-inflammatory olive, avocado, and coconut oils as well as omega-3s—are anti-inflammatory and included in a ketogenic diet.

Your best defense is to focus on the lifestyle choices that have been shown to reduce risk.

BOTTOM LINE: There are multiple benefits for ketogenic living.

MYTH 2: EATING FAT WILL MAKE YOU FAT AND WILL CLOG YOUR ARTERIES.

There are no known studies which prove that consuming dietary fat makes us fat, even though most of us grew up with that belief. That being said, there are some fats we should avoid.

Omega-6 fatty acids found in vegetable oils (canola, sunflower, corn, soybean, etc.) are highly inflammatory and are not good for us.

Inflammation is the body's response to infections and injuries and part of how our body heals itself. But we get into trouble when our bodies have chronic or long-term inflammation when there is no injury. For example, in blood vessels, chronic inflammation leads to the buildup of plaque. The body responds and tries to fix the problem with more inflammatory cells, which in turn cause more plaque. As this continues, the artery wall thickens, creating the probability of a cardiac event. It's chronic inflammation, not fat, that clogs arteries.

BOTTOM LINE: Eat healthy fats and avoid vegetable, seed, and soybean oil.

MYTH 3: EATING A KETO DIET WILL INCREASE CHOLESTEROL.

Modern science reveals that inflammation, not heightened cholesterol, is the cause of coronary artery disease. The amount of cholesterol in our body isn't an issue. The danger lies in the ratios of triglycerides, HDL (high-density lipoprotein), CRP (C-reactive protein, the marker for inflammation in the bloodstream), and A1C (the three-month average of our blood glucose levels). Luckily, ketogenic living is known for lowering triglycerides, raising HDL, and lowering CRP and A1C!

It's important to note that keto can temporarily raise cholesterol, but you should see a significant decrease after six months. If your doctor suggests drugs for high cholesterol, do some research (I recommend *The Great Cholesterol Myth: Why Lowering Your Cholesterol Won't Prevent Heart Disease* by Jonny Bowden and Stephen Sinatra and *Cholesterol Clarity* by Jimmy Moore), question the advice, and even seek a second opinion.

IN A NUTSHELL: Cholesterol-lowering medications are draining our brains of the cholesterol it needs. Educate yourself on why your body needs cholesterol.

MYTH 4: A CALORIE IS A CALORIE.

Calories come from the three main macronutrients—protein, carbohydrates, and fats—and they're all processed differently by our body. The main difference comes from the carb side of things. Digestible carbs get turned into sugar, which is composed of glucose and fructose. Glucose can be metabolized within all of the body's tissues, but fructose is a different story. Fructose can only be metabolized in the liver, turning it into fat, which it then sends out into our bloodstream. This is the fat that settles into our arteries and becomes deadly plaque.

NUTRIENT ANALYSIS: All calories are NOT the same.

MYTH 5: OUR BODIES NEED CARBS.

There are essential vitamins and nutrients, essential fatty acids, and essential amino acids (the building blocks of protein), but there is no such thing as an essential carbohydrate.

It's true that the brain needs glucose, but the body is very capable of taking this needed glucose from dietary protein in a process called gluconeogenesis (GNG). This process is always happening in your body, but its rate can increase or decrease depending on the health of your metabolic state. During GNG, glucose is made by breaking down other compounds such as amino acids, glycerol, lactate, glutamine, and alanine.

A brain running on ketones instead of carbohydrates experiences, among other things, better cognition, mental acuity, and focus, and mood improvement.

BOTTOM LINE: There are no essential carbs.

MYTH 6: KETO SHOULD ONLY BE DONE FOR A SHORT PERIOD OF TIME.

Due to the short- and long-term health benefits, ketogenic living is a great life plan. There is absolutely no reason a well-formulated ketogenic diet cannot be followed for life.

THE TAKEAWAY: Keto living is healthy over the long term.

MYTH 7: THE KETO DIET IS INCOMPLETE AND WILL RESULT IN MALNOURISHMENT.

The keto diet means different things to different people. It is possible to stay in ketosis by eating hot dogs and margarine, but that is a one-way street to a dangerous, nutrient-deficient diet and is not fulfilling what true keto is about. A well-formulated keto diet includes healthy fats, proteins, nuts, occasional berries, dairy, and plenty of green, leafy, and fibrous vegetables. Carbs, which are nonessential, are the only macronutrient missing from the ketogenic diet.

The trace minerals found in grains are found in bigger concentrations in meats, dairy, and other keto-available foods. Some may argue that vitamin deficiency comes from not eating enough fruit, yet there is more Vitamin C in broccoli and Brussels sprouts than is found in an orange.

THE VERDICT: Eat well-balanced, nutrient-rich keto foods and all your bases will be covered.

MYTH 8: DRINKING ALCOHOL WHILE ON KETO IS A NO-NO.

While going on a bender or a drinking binge is not recommended, having a well-deserved alcoholic beverage at the end of the week can be a part of your keto plan. Stick to clear or lighter coloured alcohol and stay away from darker versions of drink, which are caramelized with sugar. Use flavour-enhanced water as mix instead of diet soft drinks, which often contain non-keto ingredients. If your preference is something carbonated, choose club soda or a carbonated water sweetened with stevia. Dry white or red wine is fine in moderation, and Prosecco and champagne are also good low-carb options. Drinks that are high in sugar and carbs, such as sweetened mix drinks and most beers, are not good choices.

Your body will burn off any alcohol in your system before burning off any body fat, so having alcohol may slow or stall your progress. Also, alcohol will most likely affect you much more as a ketonian, so take it easy! Consider yourself a lightweight when it comes to alcohol.

THE DRINK ORDER: Easy does it and choose wisely.

MYTH 9: IT'S OKAY TO CHEAT ON KETO.

Unlike other diets, where cheat days might be encouraged to give you a mental break, cheating on the keto diet can cause you to transition out of ketosis. Ketosis is a metabolic state, and cheating could affect your metabolism and contribute to the yo-yo effect of dieting.

Eating carbs similar to a Western diet and fats similar to a keto way of eating can become a cocktail of trouble for you and your cardiovascular system.

Cheating or "celebrating" by having carb-laden foods on a keto lifestyle is the equivalent of somebody who is celebrating the six-month anniversary of quitting smoking by having a cigarette. It's counterproductive to your end goal and just plain doesn't make sense. Instead of cheating, you're better off finding a keto equivalent to what you're craving.

THE TRUTH: Just don't do it; it will hurt you in the long run.

MYTH 10: KETO IS THE SAME FOR MEN AND WOMEN.

It's one of the great injustices in this world—men lose weight quicker than women.

Here are a few reasons this happens.

Estrogen. Men and women both have estrogen in their bodies, but women have about 11 percent more. Because of the extra estrogen, women may have a harder time losing fat than men.

Muscle. Because of higher testosterone levels, most men carry more weight in muscle than most women do. The extra muscle gives men a bigger boost in their metabolic rate and helps them burn more fat.

Stress. Women tend to stress about things more than men do, and with stress comes cortisol, the stress hormone. Cortisol can cause our cells to become resistant to insulin, which in turn can lead to a rise in blood sugars and weight gain.

THE ADVICE: Don't sweat it! It's best not to compare somebody else's journey to your own. Keep making good choices and keto on.

MYTH 11: KETOSIS CAN DEVELOP INTO LIFE-THREATENING KETOACIDOSIS.
Ketosis is a metabolic state that occurs when the body switches from burning carbohydrates to burning ketones for fuel.

Ketoacidosis or DKA (diabetic ketoacidosis) occurs when a type-1 diabetic is unable to regulate ketone production due to an inability to produce insulin. Alcoholism and extreme starvation may also cause this to occur. Diabetic ketoacidosis occurs in less than 1 percent of type-1 diabetics annually.

BOTTOM LINE: Unless you're a type-1 diabetic, this is not something you have to worry about.

THE FINAL SAY

Please, don't just take my word for all this. Dig in and do your own research and come to your own conclusions. I'm not in the position to give you medical advice. These are only my opinions and my learning and thinking, formed from doing my own research and from my own personal experience.

Our first advice is to check with your health-care provider before starting any new regime. If you find your doctor is totally against ketogenic living, they may just be lacking the proper information to be able to assess your request. We recommend bringing along some well-researched articles to share with your doctor, just in case. Many health-care professionals are just learning about keto and low-carb living.

You will never change your life until you change something that you do daily. The secret to your success is found in your daily routine.

GETTING STARTED

We think the best approach is to start simple and smart. In the beginning, don't worry about the big picture and all the items you have to remove from your diet—that can be overwhelming. Just do the best you can to reduce the amount of carbs you consume.

Don't think about what can happen in a month or in a year. Just focus on the twenty-four hours in front of you and do what you can to get closer to where you want to be.

Every step you take to reduce carbs is positive and will directly impact your health. Ease back slowly. Don't try to do it all at once. Start with cutting the basics: bread, pasta, sugar. This will not only ease you into this change mentally, but it will also prepare your body for what is about to come. Start by choosing a particular carbohydrate source and removing it from your diet. Once you've conquered that, move on to the next carb, and so on until you've cut your intake to where you want to be. You don't have to start perfectly—just start!

Every step you make toward low carb and keto are great ones for you and your body. This is a learn-as-you-go process. Strive for progress, not perfection.

COUNTING CARBS

We recommend to go low carb for a week, so 50 grams or under of carbohydrates daily. That gets your body and your head used to the fact that your diet is changing. You might just decide to stay there and follow a low-carb way of eating.

The generally accepted model for a well-formulated ketogenic lifestyle involves consuming a daily lower-carb (twenty grams or less), moderate-protein, and high-fat diet. Most of your carbs will come from eating dark green and leafy veggies.

In the keto world, some people count total carbs and others count net carbs—it's a personal preference. "Net" means carbohydrates minus fibre and sugar alcohols. In regard to sugar alcohols, there are two schools of thought. Some subtract them all and others only subtract half if the amount is over five grams.

These different counting methods exist because of the uncertainty in how much of these sugar alcohols are absorbed by the body and how much is treated as waste. There is no way to quantify the breakdown of the numbers. You just have to figure out which works best for you based on your own ketogenic values. Personally, I'm on the stricter side of the keto world, and in my opinion, the possibility of extra carbs is a risk that's too great to take. I'm a net carb girl, so I use caution with sugar alcohols. I measure using half the count if over five grams. (See Appendix B for more information about sugar alcohols.)

PROTEIN

Your next priority after cutting carbs is to ensure you're getting enough protein, usually 60 to 110 grams daily. There is a myth in the keto world that if you eat too much protein it will take you out of ketosis. This should not be a concern, unless you eat massive amounts of protein daily. Generally, the rule of thumb is to eat the same amount of protein you did in your pre-keto days, just choose fattier cuts of meat, keeping in mind that you are also getting protein from many vegetable sources (e.g., broccoli, asparagus, Brussels sprouts, kale, spinach, and cauliflower).

HEALTHY FATS

The hardest part of keto is getting your head around the high-fat part. Don't fear the fat. Use healthy fats to satisfy your hunger and provide your body with a new source of energy. Don't try to force-feed yourself fats! Keto is not about guzzling bacon juice. Instead, realize that healthy fats are what will keep you satisfied, so try to incorporate them into your meals and snacks for the day.

GOOD FATS VS BAD FATS

Choose healthy fats like avocado, coconut oil, MCT oil, and extra virgin olive oil (EVOO). Stay away from low-quality vegetable oils. They are inflammatory and aren't really made from vegetables at all; they are made by processing seeds with chemicals and heat. They are not your friend.

GOOD FATS

Butter
Coconut Oil
Bacon Fat
Tallow
Lard
Palm Oil
Olive Oil
Avacado Oil
Fish Oil
Ghee

Vegetable Oil
Margarine
Corn Oil
Canola Oil
Sunflower Oil
Safflower Oil
Grapeseed Oil
Soybean Oil
Shortening

BAD FATS

We recommend using an app or other food tracker to calculate your personal macros and how they translate into what your day should look like food-wise. You download the app, sign up for an account, and from there the app will walk you through finding your own macros. Your macros will be 5 percent carbs, 25 percent protein, and 70 percent fats. What that looks like in grams will be different for everybody. These values are calculated from your own personal data (current weight, activity level, age, height, etc.).

We used and recommend My Fitness Pal. The interface is easy to understand and it also allows for weight and exercise to be added to your daily journal. Other apps are Senza, Carb Manager, and Chronometer, to name a few. Selection of app depends on your own preference for style and ease of use. A word of caution here: you will find multiple entries for most food selections within these apps. Most of the food entries are input by the app users, so exercise common sense when choosing your food entry. If it looks too good to be true, it probably is.

Our recommendation is to start off tracking until you get a sense of what your ideal food day on the ketogenic way of eating looks like. Then decide if you want to track long-term or not.

25%
PROTEIN

5%
CARBS

KETO
MACROS

70%
FATS

 Pick up a food scale to accurately measure your daily food intake.

CAPTURE THE BEFORE

Take measurements. This is highly recommended for brand-new ketonians. You will find that the scales are NOT your friend, and much of the time you will be losing inches but that stubborn scale won't budge. This is normal! You don't have to share these measurements with anyone, but take them. You can't always depend on the scales to give you an accurate picture; one glance at a side-by-side comparison of measurements can give you a better picture of your progress.

Take "before" pictures—a head shot, full front-on head to toe, and full side-on head to toe. Start a private file on your phone or computer to track your progress. Sometimes we can't see our own progress in the mirror, but photos don't lie. These shots are for you to watch your progress, so let it all hang out. This is not the time to suck in your belly. Nobody will see them, unless you choose to share them when you're well on your way to the ideal you.

KEEP IT SIMPLE, SWEETHEART

The most crucial time is the first few weeks. It's the time that you reset your metabolism and help your body learn how to heal itself. This is the time for super clean eating. Stick with healthy fats, protein, and green leafy vegetables. Stay away from the chemicals, starches, and sugars, and also from fancy keto recipes and snacks. First-timers to keto usually make the mistake of jumping on the "fancy recipe" bandwagon. Fat bombs, pork rinds, and keto snacks are all things for further down the road. You have lots of time for fancy meals; for now, follow the KISS guidelines: Keep It Simple, Sweetheart.

> Don't give up on your goal because of one setback. You don't slash your other tires because you have one flat tire.

It's all about getting back to basics. Most of us have been feeding our body chemicals and overloading it with sugar, and we've never learned to listen to what our body is trying to tell us. It's time to detox, give your body a break, and cut the dietary crap. Eat real whole food and stay clear of packaged or processed food. The more a food is processed, the more you should stay away.

For the first little while, keeping it simple also means avoiding recipes with almond and coconut flours. Even though they are keto acceptable, they are still quite carby and tend to give many of us a bloated feeling. Save those recipes for later down the road and, even then, only as an occasional thing. These items should not be everyday foods.

You will stumble and falter—that's normal—it's something we all do. The mindset we need to adopt is: "If I stumble seven times, I get up eight times." The main thing is not to wallow or beat yourself up during these times. Pick yourself up, dust yourself off, and get right back on that horse. You are making good choices for yourself. You are making progress.

You can do this. Keto on.

YES, WE KNOW YOU HAVE CRAVINGS

A craving, also called selective hunger, is the desire to consume a specific food. While some cravings are the result of missing nutrients within your body, those cases are rare. Most cravings are 100 percent superficial and you CAN get past them. They are often a sign of boredom and stem from your "sugar fuel" days. When you eat sugar or glucose, your body quickly uses that sugar (read: insulin spike then crash) and your body wants more, much like an alcoholic wants more alcohol. Your brain has become conditioned to the "happy hormones" released every time sugar is present.

The next time you feel a craving, ask yourself, is this hunger psychological or physical? If it's psychological, give yourself a gentle nudge to move on. If it's physical, give your body the nutrients it needs, not empty calories. Adopt the theory that, for this first while at least, you are eating to live, not living to eat. There is a big difference.

FINDING A NEW BLISS POINT

When most of us think back on our lifelong careers of overeating, we can recall a food item or two that we just couldn't get enough of. Whether it's that "bet you can't eat just one" salty snack or that chocolaty sweet dream you can't resist, in most cases we're talking about something that was produced to keep you wanting more and more.

Let me introduce you to a new term: bliss point. Bliss point is the point in a processed food where it is as delicious as it can possibly be without making you feel satisfied or full. Food manufacturers use the bliss point to test and tweak products to keep you eating and craving.

Manufacturers primarily use three elements in combination—salt, sugar, and fat—to hit all of our taste buds in a perfect way and send a "We need more!" message to our brains. Natural food hits our pleasure receptors with these same three ingredients, but today's science has created that perfect ratio that makes us crave our favourite snacks in a way that is similar to an addiction. Food producers utilize market research, focus groups, and taste tests over and over until they achieve their goal, perfecting their products' bliss point and driving their sales and profit through the roof.

We usually advise people who are new to the world of keto to totally cut out sweets and go back to the basics for the first couple of months. One of our goals as ketonians is to find a new sweet spot or bliss point. We must acknowledge that those daily spoonfuls of sugar are part of the problem that caused us to want to start a keto diet in the first place. You have to slow down and learn to walk before you can run. Let your body detox and just forget about all those eating habits that got you into trouble. We understand your body has cravings—every person who goes through a detoxification has cravings. It's your body signalling that it's used to having something. But those cravings were not helpful in your old life and they won't be helpful in this keto way of eating. Don't let yourself be a slave to food.

I promise you, if you forego that sweet treat for just a couple of weeks, you will be absolutely amazed at how sweet the simplest item actually tastes. As you work on yourself, don't forget to work on your bliss point! It's truly a part of the healthier you that you're searching for.

KETO FOOD GUIDELINES

There is so much to learn about our new way of eating—no wonder so many people get overwhelmed! Sometimes all we really need to know is what we can eat. I remember in our early days, faithful sidekick and hubby Geoff's line was, "Just tell me what to eat!"

Here are our suggestions for which foods to eat and which you should avoid.

The general rule of thumb for vegetables is, if it grows below the ground, it is starchier and not keto friendly; the exception is turnip, in moderation. Vegetables that grow above the ground are "keto good"; an exception is peas, which are high in sugars and therefore not recommended on a keto diet.

Berries are the only keto-friendly fruit, in moderation. If you're going to step outside of this and have other fruit, eat the real fruit, not juice. There is more fibre in the fruit and the fibre will counteract some of the sugars.

Milk is full of sugar. The average 12-ounce glass has 17-20 grams of carbs, depending on the brand. Other dairy items are okay, as long as there are no starches or chemicals added.

If you're used to milk in your coffee and you can't go without, try bulletproof coffee (BPC) instead. Most recipes for BPC use a combination of whipping cream, butter, and sweetener, but you can use any combination of these ingredients. Read more about it in our recipe for Bulletproof Coffee (page 82).

> If they took sugar and hidden sugars from your local grocery store, over 80% of the store's food would be gone!

KEEP AN EYE OUT FOR THESE HIDDEN SUGARS:

	corn sweetener	glucose	molasses
	corn syrup	glucose solids	muscovado
agave necta	corn syrup solids	golden sugar	panocha
Barbados sugar	crystalline fructose	golden syrup	raw sugar
barley malt	date sugar	grape sugar	refiner's syrup
beet sugar	demerara sugar	high fructose corn syrup (HFCS)	rice syrup
brown sugar	dextran	honey powdered	sorbitol
buttered syrup	dextrose	sugar	sorghum syrup
cane crystals	diastase	invert sugar	starch
cane juice	diastatic malt	lactose malt	sucralose
cane sugar	ethyl maltol	malt syrup	sucrose
caramel	fructose	maltodextrin	syrup
carob syrup	fruit juice	maltose	treacle
castor sugar	fruit juice concentrate	mannitol	turbinado sugar
coconut sugar	galactose	maple syrup	yellow sugar

Get some natural sea or Himalayan pink salt for increased sodium. Sodium is one of the main electrolytes our bodies require for survival. Table salts have gone through a chemical process that removes most of the natural elements, including sodium and other minerals that are deficient in our bodies. Sea salt and Himalayan pink salt are 98 percent sodium and are full of trace elements that our body can use. (Himalayan salt is also the only salt known to lower blood pressure.)

In the early days of keto, your body goes through a diuretic process, using the water in your body to shuttle out toxins and other items that have been stored over the years, including electrolytes (sodium, potassium, and magnesium), and these electrolytes need to be replaced. (Because your body uses water to facilitate this cleansing, you will notice you are thirstier than normal; this requires that you increase the amount of water you drink.) Don't overthink this, just drink to thirst.

Check all nutritional labels and ingredient lists, and educate yourself on all the different names for sugar and starches. Be prepared to find them everywhere. Practice due diligence on every single thing that goes in your mouth, including medicines, vitamins, gum, etc. Check it all! Look for trigger words such as *modified* and prefixes such as *poly*. If a food has unknown ingredients that sound overly complicated, it's probably best to avoid.

Many new ketonians don't realize that keto is ingredients first, meaning even before counting carbs, quality of food is the most important thing to watch for while on a ketogenic diet. The more you check labels, the more chemicals you will see. Chemicals harm our body; they should be avoided in our food. Aim for foods with a very small ingredients list and avoid processed ingredients in food. Even better, look for foods that don't have a list of ingredients (e.g., meats from the butcher, veggies, berries).

For foods that have an ingredients list, less is always better. The more ingredients/components in a commercially available food, the more chance there is of having additives or chemicals that are not a part of ketogenic living. If I pick up a product that has a list of ingredients that's a mile long, I don't even bother to check out how many carbs it has. I just know it's not for me!

"Think about it: if there is a 'health food' section in the grocery store, what does that make the rest of the food sold there?" —Dr. Mark Hyman

ARE YOU IN KETOSIS?

Everybody's journey through ketosis is different. Some will successfully reach ketosis in days, while others might take weeks, depending on how successful the individual is at removing carbohydrates from their diet. Even the signs and symptoms of ketosis will vary from person to person.

THE JOURNEY THROUGH KETOSIS

 WEEK [1]

- → Glycogen stores deplete within 24 hours of cutting carbs.
- → Gluconeogenesis begins to fuel our brains with needed glucose.
- → By Day 3, ketones are being produced.
- → Energy highs and lows are experienced as the body begins to switch between fuels.
- → Initial water weight is lost.

 WEEK [2]

- → Sodium flush accelerates the loss of potassium as our body begins to detoxify and heal.
- → Keto flu symptoms may start here.
- → With the lack of carbs, blood glucose levels begin to lower and stabilize.
- → Ketones are spilled as they are being produced faster than they can be used.
- → With the help of gluconeogenesis the brain becomes more effective at using ketones for fuel.

 WEEK [3]

- → The body becomes more efficient at burning ketones, making urine strips less effective in testing for ketosis.
- → Keto flu symptoms begin to lessen.

 WEEK [4]

- → The liver increases bile production to help break down fats, the gallbladder stores more bile, and the pancreas begins to produce more enzymes to help with fat burning.
- → Blood cholesterol level starts to increase as more weight is lost.

 WEEK [6] (PLUS)

- → Fat adaptation and metabolic adaptation complete. Your body now prefers to burn ketones over glucose.
- → Increased and steady energy levels.
- → Decrease in hunger.
- → Health improvements ramp up.
- → Weight losses are typically between 1 and 2 pounds a week.

Some people resort to monitors to let them know if they're in ketosis. Keto sticks are a common topic on ketogenic forums, but these are unreliable at best. They are not meant to tell you if you're in ketosis but rather to let you know that your body is releasing ketones. These keto sticks will become even more unreliable when you become fat adapted. There are also blood and breath monitors that can be purchased. While these are more reliable, they can be expensive, especially if you have to buy test strips.

The best way to know if you are in ketosis is to read your body's signals. Slow down and notice what your body is telling you—it's giving you all the information you need to know if you're doing well in ketosis.

The following are the most common, short-lived signs that you are entering ketosis.

1. **FREQUENT URINATION**
2. **DRY MOUTH**
3. **BAD BREATH**
4. **ENERGY HIGHS AND LOWS**
5. **DIGESTIVE ISSUES**
6. **BODY ODOUR**

Sometimes if you're not successful in reaching ketosis, it's just a matter of tweaking your meal plan. Ketogenic living is a learn-as-you-go process, and there is much to learn.

 Even after weeks or months into this way of eating, recheck the labels on any products you're using. Anything that has "uglies" (i.e., hidden starches, sugars, chemicals) needs to be in the trash.

MY EXPERIENCE ENTERING KETOSIS

I took baby steps and eased myself into the world of keto. Right from the get-go, I felt fabulous! As I made the jump from low-carb to full-on keto, there were so many health gains, I quickly became convinced that there really was something to this keto/low-carb thing.

Then it hit. I was sitting in the living room with Hubby and Pa and I realized that I felt nauseated. I didn't think a lot of it at that point, I just put it down to an upset tummy. Then when I stood up, the nausea was accompanied by the oddest feeling of being off-kilter. I wouldn't describe it as being dizzy or light-headed, it was more an airy feeling in my head and a sensation that something was not right. I quickly asked Mr. Google about keto side effects and stumbled upon an article about "keto flu" and with it, the suggestion of drinking a cup of broth for temporary relief.

Easy. Done. And fixed.

A couple of days later, it hit again. Hubby and I were running errands at lunchtime. He was about to go back to work and I was to continue on with the vehicle by myself. This time the off-kilter feeling was multiplied by the sensation of pressure in my head, as though someone was squishing my forehead and narrowing my field of vision. This weird headache affected me so much that I hung onto Geoff's side for balance. I realized that I couldn't function like this, and I certainly couldn't drive. We stopped at a grocery store and bought a litre of broth. I drank it in the car as Hubby drove. By the time we reached his drop-off point, I was feeling well enough to drive. This second bout gave me a new resolve to figure out keto flu.

WHAT IS KETO FLU?

Some people transition seamlessly into a keto way of eating without experiencing any "flu" symptoms. If your diet leans toward healthy, you may only encounter mild keto flu symptoms or none at all. Some people are naturally metabolically flexible, which means they can shift metabolic states easily without experiencing health symptoms.

For most, the keto flu usually starts at about the 24 to 48-hour point and lasts a week and can last up to a month. Not only can we assure you that these keto flu symptoms will pass, we can also offer suggestions to get you through it quickly. We suggest you start these actions before the keto flu even strikes. Nip it in the bud before it happens.

Let's take a quick look at why the keto flu happens. Up until this point your body has been burning glucose to survive. When you start a low-carb or keto lifestyle, you restrict carbohydrates and your body must learn how to burn its backup energy source: fat.

Water and sodium flush. When you restrict carbs, your insulin levels drop, which signals your kidneys to release sodium. This sodium flush is part of your body's detox or cleansing and can cause losses of up to ten pounds of weight as water delivers sodium, potassium, and magnesium (electrolytes) out of your body. (Yes, I'm sorry, that big initial weight loss is water weight and part of the keto transition, but don't be discouraged; it's a great first step. As long as you stay away from the carbs, this water weight will stay away.)

Furthermore, when you start a ketogenic diet, the glycogen, or glucose, stored in your body gets burned up rather quickly, taking with it the water it was stored in. The drop in glycogen and insulin levels can also cause symptoms such as dizziness, nausea, muscle cramping, and headaches.

Also, most of the processed foods that you were eating pre-keto were full of sodium. As you transition to keto, your body will miss those added salts. That's a second reason that your body is both asking for and needs extra salt.

Decreased thyroid levels. Dietary carbohydrates and thyroid function are closely connected, so when you cut carbs, thyroid levels can also fall. This hormone helps to regulate your body's temperature, metabolism, and heart rate. Brain fog and fatigue are also part of this thyroid adjustment.

Increased cortisol levels. A ketogenic diet tells your body that big changes are happening, and your body's initial response is to panic. This panic triggers the production of cortisol, the stress hormone. Mood swings, irritability, and insomnia are sure signs that cortisol levels are changing in your system.

KETO FLU SYMPTOMS

sugar cravings	nausea
dizziness	muscle soreness/cramps
brain fog/headache	difficulty falling asleep
lack of concentration/confusion	chills
irritability/moodiness	sore throat
stomach pains/cramping	heart flutters/arrhythmia

STEPS TO MANAGE KETO FLU

Don't try to push past the keto flu! Correct it!

1. REPLACE ELECTROLYTES

Ts your body rids itself of toxins via sodium flush (electrolytes), you're left feeling unsteady. The symptoms you are feeling are your body screaming on a cellular level, telling you it needs electrolytes replenished.

Potassium, magnesium, and sodium are the main elements of electrolytes. If your electrolytes aren't balanced, your body will not feel right.

Never supplement potassium without consulting with your doctor, as there can be cardiac implications. Instead, eat fish, meat, leafy greens, and winter squash. If you are battling cramps, constipation, or muscle weakness, seek out potassium-rich foods.

For magnesium, eat spinach, chicken, beef, or fish, or supplement with 300-500mg per day. Magnesium glycinate is the recommended and most bio-available formula. Magnesium helps with keto flu symptoms like muscle cramps, dizziness, and fatigue.

It is particularly important to supplement sodium, as keto is a natural diuretic. We recommend using Himalayan pink salt or natural sea salt.

> Some people take an electrolyte supplement at least once per day. Commercial electrolyte drinks contain processed sugar and chemicals and are not recommended. Avoid these by making your own keto-friendly sports drink at home using 1 cup of water, 1 tsp Himalayan salt, and freshly squeezed lemon or lime juice.

2. HYDRATE

Drink to thirst! Don't over-hydrate, as you can flush out electrolytes when excessive water is consumed. Staying hydrated will help relieve headaches and boost your energy levels when you're feeling sluggish. Set a "hydration alarm" on your phone to help you remember, and keep a full glass or bottle of water within reach at all times.

3. DRINK BONE BROTH

Bone broth adds a serving of water and electrolytes to your diet, which will offset some of the discomfort you feel. Make your own broth by simmering bones for hours (see our Bone Broth recipe, page 105).

4. EAT MORE FAT

Supplementing with healthy fats such as coconut oil, avocado oil, extra virgin olive oil, butter, or MCT (medium-chain triglycerides) oil may help you avoid keto flu altogether.

> Keto flu can happen at any time, especially if you're incorporating fasting in your regime. Take care with your supplements through every step of your keto journey.

5. EXERCISE GENTLY

Mild exercise such as yoga, gentle walks, or meditation can help relieve muscle pain and tension and release endorphins to help boost your mood and motivation.

6. EAT CLEAN

Keto is not just about cutting carbs. It's also about eating clean. Go out of your way to cut chemicals and toxins, and stay away from processed foods. Remember, you are teaching your body to recalibrate. Feed it the best fuel you can at this time.

7. GET LOTS OF SLEEP

A good night's sleep can help conquer keto flu by keeping your cortisol levels in check. Try for seven to nine hours a night. You may want to brew a keto-friendly tea with herbs such as chamomile, valerian root, and lavender. These have a calming effect on your nervous system. Cut off the use of electronics at least two hours before you go to bed. The blue light from these devices interferes with your ability to fall asleep.

8. UP YOUR CARBS

If all else fails, up your healthy carb intake (i.e., veggies). Sometimes we try to force the change just a little too quickly. Adding a few carbohydrates back into your diet gives your body the chance to adjust and eases the overall transition.

ARE YOU FAT ADAPTED?

Your next exciting stage is fat adaptation, where your body turns itself into the human equivalent of a locomotive train, one that has no problem staying on the tracks, efficiently burns its own fat for fuel, and is on its way to being healthy, happy, and slim.

A lot of people get confused between being in ketosis and being fat adapted, but there is a distinct difference between the two. It's relatively easy to get into ketosis. Getting fat adapted takes a little longer.

At the start of your journey toward ketosis, your body doesn't yet understand that you've actively chosen a new lifestyle—it thinks there is just a momentary lapse in its normal fuel supply. As it realizes it has no carbs or sugars to utilize, it reaches for fat as a fuel, but it doesn't understand that fat can be its primary source of fuel. You have transitioned to ketosis, where your body is producing ketones but is not yet efficient at burning or using them. That requires being fat adapted.

Fat adaptation usually comes after you have been in ketosis for a constant period, about six weeks, though it can take up to six months to reach adaptation. At this point, your body has become more efficient and prefers to burn fat over glucose and has built up enzymes to help burn fats. When fat adaptation occurs, not only will you feel great all the time, you will also stop craving carbs. You will feel satisfied.

The transition period from keto to fat adapted is *the* most important stage of ketosis. Not only are you teaching your body to switch fuels, you are resetting your damaged metabolism. If you are in ketosis and you're still craving carbs, it's a sure sign that you're not yet fat adapted. Some ketonians never reach this phase because they give in to little cheats, thinking that "it won't hurt this one time" and that it's okay to eat this one little thing. This mentality will keep you from achieving what ketogenic living is really about. It will keep you on the outskirts of the keto world, never really fulfilling your potential.

It's incredibly important to eat clean every day. Not doing so will hold you back from achieving fat adaptation and reaching your health and weight-loss goals.

Keto is not a diet; it's a constant metabolic state where you have healed your body and trained it to process fats for fuel.

WHAT CAN I DO TO ENSURE I GET ADAPTED TO BURNING FAT?

Don't fear the fat. This is the single biggest mistake people make when they start keto. They fill their bowls with what Sidekick Geoff calls rabbit food: lettuce and celery and cabbage. They mistakenly believe this is the way they "diet" to lose weight. Keto is not a diet. While vegetables are a part of any healthy and balanced way of eating, in order to be successful with keto you also need to eat healthy fats that will satisfy you and keep you feeling full. This is a high-fat, moderate-protein, low-carb way of eating. Veggies fall in the carb portion of the menu, and they will not keep you feeling full. Healthy fats fill that role.

Increase your healthy fats. Add butter over the top wherever you can, eat avocado, increase olive and avocado oils whenever possible, choose the fattiest cuts of meats. If you get the carbs down where they should be and the fat up to where it should be, your body will feel satisfied.

Stay away from fancy keto recipes, **keto ingredients**, **and keto sweets**. Your body needs to detoxify, and if you just switch from one version of treat foods to another, you're asking for an upside-down metabolism. Eat healthy fats, proteins (fatty cuts of meat), and moderate leafy greens. Period.

Don't have even a tiny little treat. You can do this. Be true to yourself and give yourself permission to do what's right for your body, for maybe the first time in your life. You have the rest of your life to have keto-friendly treats—for now let your body transition. Tighten your belt and stand firm at "no thank you"!

Concentrate on eating clean, eliminating toxins, and cutting and counting carbs.

HOW DO I KNOW I'M FAT ADAPTED?

Most people have difficulty knowing when they've reached this mecca of fat-burning metabolism. Many flock to keto strips to find their answer. Keep in mind that as you become fat adapted, your body learns to use most or all of the ketones you're producing, causing the amount of ketones in your urine to decrease drastically or even disappear. Testing blood or breath is a more accurate way to check for ketones. But the real proof that you're fat adapted is in the following signs:

Food cravings disappear. Not only that, your body will start to desire the type of foods that you have become accustomed to while on a ketogenic diet.

Appetite settles. Once you become fat adapted, you're no longer hungering for food in the same way as before and you can go for long periods without eating. This is the time when people generally begin to experiment with fasting as you lose those hunger sensations that ruled your life before keto.

Energy level stabilizes. Sidekick Geoff explains this best in relation to his work day. In his pre-keto days, he often ate bread or oatmeal for breakfast and a sandwich for lunch. About an hour or two after eating, he would experience a major energy drain and a slump in mental clarity, and he was just dang cranky. Most times by three o'clock he would hit the vending machine for another round of carbs to fuel him until he got home from work.

His new keto day has him breaking his overnight fast mid-to-late morning by enjoying a small high-fat meal of bacon and eggs with lots of butter and Himalayan salt. This gives him a consistent level of energy, mood, and mental focus, which allows him to sail through his day, satisfied and hunger free.

Mental clarity improves. Most of us struggle daily, not only with decreased mental clarity, but also an inability to *stay in the moment*. All those carbs have our thinking process scattered and our focus all over the place. Fat adaptation and ketosis allow our minds to settle, and we feel like our cognitive abilities improve sharply.

Quality of sleep improves. This was a big one for me. My past life was full of fitful nights where I spent the entire night "in the rats," as I called it. From the moment I closed my eyes to the moment I opened them in the morning, I ran from dream to dream in a drowsy state of confusion. Now I close my eyes and my body and mind go clunk every night. I fall into a deep, satisfying slumber. I awaken in the morning refreshed and feeling great.

> Magnesium supplements are an additional help with sleep issues. Magnesium is known to calm the nervous system and helps most people get a deeper, calmer night's sleep.

Those are just some of the benefits to being fat adapted—the list goes on. Being fat adapted also gives you a bit more flexibility in the amount of carbs you can consume on a daily basis. For the most part, as long as you stay within 50 grams or less of carbohydrates a day, you should remain in a ketogenic state. If you do happen to eat more carbs than your body will tolerate, it can usually burn off the extra quickly and go right back to ketosis without missing a beat.

KETOGENIC LIVING: BEYOND CUTTING SUGAR

Some people assume that keto is only about dropping the sugar (i.e., carbs), but it's about more than that. Yes, it's about controlling your glucose and insulin responses, but it's also about eating foods that reduce inflammation and eliminating food that can inflame your system. It's about eating food that will decrease fluctuations in hormones. It's about clean eating and getting chemicals out of our bodies.

Once you've managed to get your carb intake down to 20 grams or less per day and have settled into that new reality, you're ready to move on to making other changes to your diet. Beyond cutting sugar, starches, and processed foods, here is a list of common foods to AVOID:

- ✖ alcohol (in excess)
- ✖ aspartame and other chemical sweeteners
- ✖ beans and lentils (exceptions: green beans and mung beans)
- ✖ cereals, including granola
- ✖ corn and corn products, including corn chips, corn syrup, and popcorn
- ✖ deli meats
- ✖ fast food
- ✖ genetically modified foods
- ✖ honey
- ✖ hot dogs (unless they're keto-friendly)
- ✖ hydrogenated and partially hydrogenated oils
- ✖ legumes
- ✖ margarine
- ✖ molasses
- ✖ muffins
- ✖ pasta
- ✖ pies and pastries
- ✖ potatoes (including French fries)
- ✖ preservatives
- ✖ rice (and rice products)
- ✖ shortening
- ✖ soda (including diet soda)
- ✖ vegetable oils
- ✖ soy (and soy products)
- ✖ sucralose and other chemical sweeteners
- ✖ wheat flour
- ✖ white bread, including bagels

And here is a list of anti-inflammatory foods, the GOOD stuff:

- ✓ asparagus
- ✓ avocado and avocado oil
- ✓ bell peppers
- ✓ black pepper
- ✓ bok choy
- ✓ broccoli
- ✓ cabbage
- ✓ cauliflower
- ✓ cayenne pepper
- ✓ chia seeds
- ✓ cinnamon
- ✓ coconut and coconut oil
- ✓ cod
- ✓ eggs
- ✓ fermented foods (e.g., sauerkraut, kimchi)
- ✓ flax seeds
- ✓ garlic
- ✓ ginger
- ✓ green beans
- ✓ hemp seeds
- ✓ kale
- ✓ leafy greens
- ✓ mackerel
- ✓ nuts
- ✓ olives and olive oil
- ✓ omega-3 fatty acids
- ✓ onion
- ✓ oysters
- ✓ rosemary
- ✓ salmon
- ✓ sardines
- ✓ spinach
- ✓ turmeric
- ✓ tuna

Remember to choose foods that don't have a list of ingredients, real foods like vegetables and fresh meat and fish, the foods your grandparents would have eaten.

Keto is not a short-term diet, it's a long-term lifestyle change.

ARE YOU KETO STALLED?

There is so much controversy over this on ketogenic forums: "You're only stalled if your weight hasn't moved in six weeks." "You're only stalled if your measurements haven't decreased by X number of inches." "You've only stalled if..."

Our take on stalling is a little different than any of those.

Keto is a journey to optimal health; weight loss is only a small part of the equation. Many of us lose weight along the way, but did you know that many people also use ketosis to gain weight? As we journey toward detoxifying our body, we should also be working toward good mental health—learning to destress and listening to our body and really becoming the best we can be. The ultimate keto journey is about getting in touch with our body and getting healthy, both mentally and physically.

Stressing over the number on the scale can have a detrimental effect. It's impossible to achieve your ideal weight when you're stressing or worrying over the details. When you're stressed, your body produces cortisol, the stress hormone, which is also the hormone responsible for storage of visceral fat. That's the nasty fat, the kind that's been identified as responsible for heart attacks and stroke. The more you stress, the more your body stores fat. It's a vicious cycle.

When you look at all the things we're working toward, it makes you wonder why so many of us quantify our success by the number on that scale. Sure, maybe that number isn't moving right now, but is your body working behind the scenes to rebuild your damaged metabolism? Are there inches falling off your measurements and are your clothes getting looser? Is your fat turning into muscle? Is your body working at detoxifying and removing chemicals and other uglies that it has been storing over the years? It's impossible to measure everything that's happening. The scale not moving can be the result of so many things—a bowel movement that hasn't happened yet; an increase/decrease in sodium; eating a meal late in the day; weighing yourself at a different time in the day; and many more reasons. Don't worry about what the scale says.

ALL ABOUT THE WHOOSH

Most people assume that weight loss is an arrow that points down and keeps going down until you reach your desired weight. In reality it's a twisty-turvy, constant, up-and-down zigzag that frustrates the heck out of most people. Weight loss can be affected by so many factors—water retention, eating a late-night meal, menstrual cycle, stress, lack of sleep, etc. No wonder most dieters get frustrated with the process and bail.

Another factor you should take into account is the whoosh factor. Yes, folks, it is a real thing. When we lose weight, the fat cells don't disappear, they just shrink up and stay in our body. That's where our old habits come back to temporarily haunt us.

For those of us who have experienced yo-yo dieting, when we start eating healthy, our body assumes we're just doing that same old thing again, and it decides to save itself some time. Assuming you're going to go back to your old ways, it holds the fat cell, filling it with water, and waits patiently. No loss is seen on the scales, as you've just had a displacement of fat for water and not an actual loss of weight.

But rest assured, you have lost fat. Eventually, as long as you stay on the plan and show your own metabolism who's boss, those fat cells will give up and collapse in a *whoosh!* In most cases you will wake up in the morning five or six pounds lighter than when you went to sleep. Fat is converted to carbon dioxide and released as you breathe. As you are snuggled away in your bed catching Zs, your body is chugging away and helping to make you healthy.

 Did you know that your body releases fat by converting it to CO2 and then exhaling it?

So again, the next time you jump on that scale, don't give too much value to the number you see. Rest assured there are positive processes happening behind the scenes. Have faith in the process. Keto works. And never forget, you're so much more than the number on that scale.

SLOW AND STEADY IS THE WAY TO GO

In all honesty, you don't want to lose the weight fast. When you go through quick weight loss, you end up with saggy excess skin that seems to be drooping off your body. Instead of coming out of your weight-loss journey looking and feeling healthy and rejuvenated, you end up looking older than you should, worn out and not healthy. Losing weight slowly and steadily gives your body time to go behind the scenes and repair some of the issues that otherwise surface with a big weight loss. Trust in the keto process and know that if you're eating less than 20 grams of carbs a day, you will lose weight. It may not happen as fast as you like. As much as you want to lose it overnight, unfortunately keto doesn't install a spigot on your body that miraculously oozes excess fat. You didn't gain the weight overnight, and you won't lose it that way either.

Find other ways to measure your success—the way your clothes fit, the compliments you receive from others—but mostly learn that it's okay to love yourself, just the way you are. We're all works in progress and often our own worst critics. If we judged our friends as harshly as we judge ourselves, we would lead pretty lonesome lives.

Eating well is a sign of self-respect.

Overall, it's important to keep in mind that you can't be natural and healthy if you've got yourself wigged out and stressed to the nines. Take several deep breaths, and get your head around the fact that anything quality takes time, and you ARE quality.

ARE YOU MAINTENANCE READY?

So, you've successfully followed the ketogenic diet and you've lost the weight. You're feeling fabulous in your new ketofied skin and you're starting to wonder what's next. How do you maintain this new keto bod? It's so easy at this point to relax and let everything backslide, but nobody wants to go back to where we started way back when.

Just as we all have our own version of what keto looks like for us, we also have our own style of maintenance. What works for somebody else may not work for you.

Here are a few maintenance tips.

Continue to limit carbs. Keep in mind this is a way of eating, not a temporary diet. If you go back to your Western diet ways, you will go back to your Western diet waistline. You can slightly increase your healthy carb level, but continue to watch your levels to see how this affects your weight.

Switch from weight loss to muscle building. Increase your activity level and start muscle training exercises. Lifting weights, working with resistance bands, or even old-fashioned physical labour can help tone your muscles and your new body. Building muscle will help increase your metabolism, which in turn will help you keep your weight off.

Increase fats. More healthy fats can be what's needed to keep you where you want to be. It's just more of the same fats that you used to reach your keto goal. And who ever complained because they have to eat more bacon?

Keep a food journal. If you stopped keeping a food journal along your keto journey, this is an important time to get active with it again. Learning how to maintain your weight is different for everyone. Tracking will help you know what foods are right for you.

Keep in mind that our body has different goals than our minds do. Just because you have chosen a certain ideal weight, your body may be comfortable at another weight altogether. Some people continue on their regular keto path for years and stay the exact same weight. Others will continue on and notice that they stop losing weight at a level that works better for their body. Be patient and allow time to find the point that feels good for you and your body.

Last but not least, we recommend finding a new goal to focus on. Now that you've reached your own weight comfort level, you need to establish a new goal to keep you on track. Whether it's mental, emotional, spiritual, or physical, find some new ways to move forward. Practice yoga, do a spinning class, pick up a new language, or learn to meditate. Keep the optimal you in the forefront by switching it up and finding even more ways to develop the ultimate you.

East Coast Keto Cooking

KITCHEN TIPS: READ BEFORE YOU COOK!

The following kitchen tips apply to food preparation in general and to the *East Coast Keto* recipes in particular.

Read your recipe in advance, then prep and organize. Timing is often crucial in recipes, and if you have to stop everything to cut an ingredient while cooking, it may impact your final results. In the cooking world this is known *mise en place*, which is French for putting everything in place. Have everything chopped, washed, and ready to roll before you turn on your stove.

Use top quality ingredients. You get out of a dish what you put in, so buy the best quality ingredients that you can.

A sharp, good-quality knife is one of the most important tools to have in the kitchen. Different knives excel at different tasks, and choosing the right one can make your work on the kitchen so much easier.

Our favourites are: an 8-inch chef's knife for general work like chopping and dicing; a paring knife for peeling and fine knife work; and a santuko knife (with indentations on the blade) for meat, fish, and veggies.

Hold the knife with your fingers tucked in under your hand like a claw. Use your knuckle as a guide for the knife, while keeping it far away from those tucked in fingers.

If you're learning knife skills, use the kitchen towel trick. Wet a kitchen or paper towel and place it under your cutting board while you work. It will keep your cutting board from moving around and might save your fingers.

Dough/pastry scrapers are your friend. Use them to quickly transfer ingredients from your cutting board to your pot.

Never overcrowd your pan or cooking dish. Food will take much longer to cook and won't get crispy. Most foods release moisture when they cook. If your food is all squished together in the pan it will steam instead of brown. Cook in several batches instead of trying to cook all at once.

Salting not only decreases the bitterness of a dish, it also helps the other ingredients play a starring role. You don't want the dish to taste salty—you just want to add enough to let the other flavours shine through.

If you add too much salt, you can dilute the liquid, add a potato (don't eat the potato!) to soak up the excess, or add more sweet or other ingredients until your dish is balanced again.

Add acid to perk up a dish. A splash of cider vinegar, wine, or lemon juice can help to intensify flavour in many dishes. Don't forget to allow it to cook for a few minutes to let it incorporate and also to burn off any alcohol.

When working with herbs, the dry version has more intense flavour than fresh herbs. Because of this, dry herbs can be added at the beginning of cooking, but save fresh herbs until the dish is almost cooked and then add them. Roll dry herbs between your hands to waken them before adding to a dish. Roll fresh herbs into a cigar shape and cut them into small ribbons. We add them to the pot after we have turned off the heat. Stir them in, wait 5 minutes, and then serve.

HERBS AND SPICES—WHAT'S THE DIFF?
Herbs are the green leaves of the plant, while spices come from the roots, bark, and seeds. Some plants have both. For example, cilantro comes from the leaves of the cilantro plant and coriander comes from the seeds of that same plant.

Cook your spices to allow the flavours to "bloom." Cooking each spice for about 30 seconds will maximize its flavour. Push any other ingredients back to the edges of the pan and add spices/herbs directly to the oil in the centre. Alternatively, toast spices on a dry pan.

The keto kitchen uses xanthan gum as a thickener instead of cornstarch or flour. Sprinkle it in a little at a time; we keep ours in a spice shaker. This is a touchy ingredient and it's easy to overdo it. The sauce (or whatever you've added it to) will continue to thicken as it cools.

Treat your meats with respect. Take them out of the fridge to bring them to room temperature before cooking. Dry/blot them with a paper towel to help them brown, and always let your meats rest after cooking. In general, steak-sized cuts rest for 3-5 minutes; roast-sized cuts should rest 10-20 minutes; large turkeys can rest for 30-90 minutes. Don't worry about the meat getting cold, especially if you're serving it with a hot sauce or gravy. Resting allows the juice to return to the core of the meat, instead of spilling out onto your cutting board.

Brown/sear your meat. People underestimate the importance of browning meat as a first step. In the cooking world, brown means flavour. So, before you put that roast in the oven, give it a dark and dirty sear on the stovetop first. Make sure the meat has been patted dry with paper towel first; wet meat will not sear. Also, keep in mind that non-stick coating prevents meat from browning properly. For a proper brown, choose a pan without non-stick coating.

Deglaze to get all those tasty burnt bits off the bottom of the pan. If brown means flavour, why leave the best of it stuck on your pan's bottom? A few dashes of acid best suits this task. The acid acts as a flavour enhancer for the dish, especially if you've added salt and it still needs an extra boost. Use vinegar, wine, or lemon to bring out this extra layer of flavour, and incorporate all those caramelized bits at the bottom of the pan as well.

Preheat your plates in the oven for hot dishes. Cold plates will chill your perfectly cooked meals. Keep food hot by warming your plates in the oven (on low) ahead of time.

· ·

To make the most of *East Coast Keto*, keep your eyes peeled for these symbols:

 Timing Tips

 Recipe Pairings & Alternative Ingredients

 Tips & Tricks

 Sidekick Comments

APPETIZERS & SNACKS

Our first run-in with avo toast happened late at night in a delightful London hotel. We had arrived in the wee hours, exhausted and half starved. After a phone call to the front desk, we found the kitchen was closed, but they would be delighted to whip us up a plate of avocado toast. A Pike family star was born!

We took this basic recipe home and played with the ingredients in our pantry. Over the years we have made many different combinations of this well-loved, classic UK dish. This trio represents our favourite combinations. Avo Toast (keto style) will help you reach your fat macros while providing you with a healthy and delicious snack.

AVO TOAST THREE WAYS   **SERVINGS** 24   **SERVING SIZE** 3 half pieces

BASIC AVO TOAST

3   slices of Tastes Like Real Bread Keto Bread (page 249), toasted

1   avocado, peeled and mashed

1   tbsp lemon juice or apple cider vinegar

1   clove of garlic, peeled and minced

Himalayan pink salt and pepper to taste

extra virgin olive oil, to finish

1. Toast Keto Bread to your desired doneness.

2. While waiting for your toast, combine avocado, lemon juice, garlic, and salt/pepper.

3. Split the avocado mix between the three pieces of toast and spread on top. Then drizzle extra virgin olive oil on top and plate.

CAPRESE AVO TOAST

Basic Avo Toast (before adding the extra virgin olive oil drizzle)

¼   cup buffalo mozzarella (or equivalent), thinly sliced

fresh basil leaves, broken into small pieces

1   medium-sized tomato, diced

White Balsamic Vinaigrette (page 253), to finish

extra virgin olive oil, to finish

fresh cracked pepper, to finish

1. Top Basic Avo Toast with slices of mozzarella and some basil with diced tomatoes on top.

2. Drizzle with our White Balsamic Vinaigrette and then olive oil, and finish with fresh cracked pepper.

PICKLED CHANTY AVO TOAST

1. Place feta strategically on the three slices of Basic Avo Toast. Try to arrange the cheese so you will have at least one piece per bite, then arrange Perfectly Pickled Chanterelles atop the feta cheese.

2. Drizzle with extra virgin olive oil and finish with Korean or red pepper flakes to taste.

Basic Avo Toast (before adding the extra virgin olive oil drizzle)

⅛ cup feta, crumbled

¼ cup Perfectly Pickled Chanterelles (page 239), or equivalent

extra virgin olive oil, to finish

Korean or red pepper flakes, to finish

ADDITIONAL VARIATIONS OF AVO TOAST

Cream Cheese, Smoked Salmon, and Red Onion | Goat Cheese and Bacon | Soft-Boiled Egg with Garam Masala | Strawberries and Balsamic | Fried Egg and Salsa | Bacon, Poached Egg, and Cheese | Turkey, Cheddar and Cranberry | Tomatoes, Charred Shrimp, and Fried Egg | Spicy Steak and Eggs | Bacon Tomato Cheese Melt with Pico de Gallo

carbs	fibre	fat	protein
17g	9g	19g	17g

This is the perfect dish to serve as an appetizer if you want to knock the socks off your guests. Serve with a bowl of Keto Cheesy Crackers (page 224) for dipping or just eat it up with a spoon right from the bowl! The layers of flavour from the bacon and the ooey gooey melted cheese tag-team with the gastrique to hit all your taste buds in the right way. And did we mention there's bacon?

With the sweet version of the gastrique (i.e., partridgeberry sauce) you could serve the Bacon-Wrapped Baked Brie for dessert. Your guests will think it's vanilla ice cream until the pairing shows off its full flavours.

BACON-WRAPPED BAKED BRIE *with* PARTRIDGEBERRY GASTRIQUE

SERVINGS 4   **SERVING SIZE** ¼ of bacon-wrapped brie

9 long slices of raw bacon

¼ tsp thyme

8 oz wheel of brie cheese

¼ cup of stevia or equivalent

Partridgeberry Gastrique
    (page 236)

1. Preheat oven to 375°F.

2. Weave together the 9 slices of bacon. (See instructions in the recipe for Bacon-Covered Meatloaf, page 142.)

3. Sprinkle thyme on the bacon weave.

4. Place wheel of brie on top of the bacon weave.

5. Sprinkle stevia on top of the brie.

6. Enclose the brie in the bacon weave, fully covering the cheese.

7. Bake for 25 minutes, until the bacon is browned and crispy.

8. Meanwhile, prepare gastrique according to instructions on page 236.

9. Remove baked brie from the oven and set aside to cool slightly (about 5 minutes).

10. Pour gastrique over the top of the warm baked brie and serve.

carbs	fibre	fat	protein
.25g	0g	34g	18.5g

Values do not include gastrique; (page 236 for details).

One of the keto struggles is finding a quick and easy, grab-and-go snack that fits within the keto way of eating. We developed Brazen Beef Jerky as a keto snack that fits in your pocket.

The key ingredient here is the Zevia soda used in the marinating process. We tried several different flavours, including black cherry, mandarin orange, root beer, cola, and lemon lime. While the rest of the flavours in the recipe dominate the subtle flavour added by the Zevia, the lemon lime is our favourite. This is such an easy snack that you can easily try them all.

We cannot stress the importance of the marinating process in this recipe. We have found 24 hours to be the ideal amount of time to allow the flavours to get infused into the meat.

We prefer to do our jerky in a dehydrator, but it can also be done in an oven on the lowest temperature setting. If Brazen Beef Jerky is something you enjoy, the low cost of an entry-level dehydrator will make preparing it even easier.

BRAZEN BEEF JERKY   SERVINGS 24   SERVING SIZE ½ OZ

1. Start by trimming most of the fat from the meat. While keto is all about highfat, jerky is best with a lower fat content on the meat.

2. Cut your meat into strips one centimetre square and the length you desire, making sure the strips are cut across the grain of the meat so there are no long stringy bits of beef. This will make for an easier bite.

3. Add all the ingredients to a bowl or large freezer bag. Place a small plate or bowl on top of the meat to weigh it down. This will ensure that all meat is thoroughly covered by the liquid.

4. Refrigerate for 12-24 hours, periodically shaking the bag or stirring contents of the bowl.

5. Remove all the strips from the marinade and pat dry with paper towel.

1 can lemon lime Zevia
2 lbs beef steak or roast
¼ cup coconut sauce
¼ cup apple cider vinegar
2 tbsp liquid smoke
1 tbsp red pepper flakes
1 tsp garlic powder
1 tsp onion powder
1 tsp paprika
½ tsp ground ginger
½ tsp black pepper

carbs	fibre	fat	protein
1.2g	0g	4g	11g

CONTINUES ▶

If your oven is at a higher temperature, you may need to slightly decrease the drying time.

FOR AN OVEN Place the marinated strips on sheet trays, then set them in the oven. Set the temperature to the lowest setting (i.e., 170°F). Turn the strips over after 3-4 hours. Return to the oven and continue to cook for approximately 1 hour or when meat is totally dehydrated.

For either method, additional or less time may be required, depending on the size of the strips.

Let the strips cool slightly, then place the pieces in an airtight bag and enjoy any time. While we recommend keeping the finished jerky in the refrigerator, it can safely be left at room temperature for extended periods of time.

FOR A DEHYDRATOR Place the marinated strips evenly over the racks. Set your dehydrator to 160°F and the time for 12 hours.

Expect a loss of at least 60 percent of the weight of your meat in the drying process. Two pounds of meat yields about twelve ounces of jerky.

This recipe works well with any nut, but our preference is the pecan.

CANDIED PECANS **SERVINGS** 16 **SERVING SIZE** 1 OZ

1. Melt butter in medium saucepan on low heat.

2. Add remaining ingredients and stir to combine.

3. Pour the mixture on a parchment-covered baking sheet.

4. Bake at 300°F for about 10 minutes, turning at the 5-minute mark.

5. Let cool.

¼ cup butter

2 cups pecans

¼ cup confectioner's Swerve or equivalent

1 tsp vanilla extract

½ tsp salt

⅓ tsp cinnamon

 Use this buttery, sweet cinnamon treat to accompany cocktails or atop salads. It can also be dressed up as a holiday gift.

carbs	fibre	fat	protein
2g	1g	12g	11g

Our first experience with fried chanties on toast was at a beach boil-up hosted by a local foraging company.

Scallops were served on hot beach rocks that had been warmed on the fire. Tea was steeped from nearby wildflowers, and chanties were served on small pieces of buttery toast. My love for foraging started that day.

Chanterelles with Bacon on Toast is our version of that same tasty treat. The foraged ingredients are replaced by ones found in our pantry, but the taste is just as delightful.

This is a quick and easy, super tasty appetizer or snack. The crispy bacon, soft meaty mushrooms, and garlicky buttered toast will hit your taste buds and make your tummy ever so happy.

CHANTERELLES with **BACON ON TOAST**

SERVINGS 4   **SERVING SIZE** 1 slice

6   strips of bacon

½ lb chanterelle mushrooms

1   clove of garlic, minced

1   tbsp apple cider vinegar

2   tbsp parsley, roughly chopped

Himalayan pink salt and freshly ground black pepper, to taste

4   pieces Tastes Like Real Bread Keto Bread (page 249), toasted and buttered

Parmesan cheese, grated, to finish

1. Sauté bacon in a large frying pan about 10-12 minutes over medium heat.

2. Add mushrooms and garlic and continue to cook for 8-10 minutes.

3. Reduce heat to low-medium and add apple cider vinegar. Simmer for 5 minutes.

4. Sprinkle with parsley, salt, and pepper.

5. Serve on toasted, buttered Keto Bread, garnished with grated cheese.

carbs	fibre	fat	protein
9.6g	4g	14g	12g

 Chanterelles with Bacon on Toast is also a great picnic option. Take along all the components in your picnic basket and combine them on site. Tastes just as good when it's cold.

Crispy Pork Belly is everything you ever loved about a pork roast, with the crispy crunchy top and the juicy and tender meat inside. You can dress this up with any type of sauce or side, but we find it stands quite easily all by itself.

Pork belly is usually cut into bacon-type slices on the shelf in the supermarket. For this recipe, you will have to request full pieces (approximately 2 inches by 2 inches by 4 inches) from the butcher or meat counter. We ask for a half pound per person cut into a slab, and cut the meat into individual portions at home, or you can ask your butcher to cut them for you.

This recipe is written for one person. Increase the ingredients proportionally per person.

CRISPY PORK BELLY   SERVING 1   SERVING SIZE 6 OZ

1. Sprinkle the spices, salt, and pepper on each piece of pork belly and transfer to a deep baking dish.

2. Roast the pork for 10-15 minutes at 425°F to crisp the outside.

3. Remove pork belly and reduce temperature to 350°F.

4. Add minced garlic to the top of the pork and return it to the oven.

5. Bake for 30 minutes or until pork reaches an internal temperature of 145°F.

6-8 oz pork belly

½   tsp cumin

½   tsp chili powder

Himalayan pink salt and pepper to taste

1   clove of garlic, minced

 For big eaters, increase the serving size to ¾ lb (12 oz) per person.

 For an extra kick, brush with Sweet Thai Chili Sauce (page 247).

carbs	fibre	fat	protein
2g	1g	90g	15.6g

Wings can be deep-fried and then tossed instead of cooked in the oven, but you won't get the same caramelization.

FOR THE WINGS

2 lbs chicken wings (about 40)

2 tbsp sesame oil

FOR THE SAUCE

1 cup chicken broth

3 tbsp hot sauce *

3 tbsp sweetener

2 tbsp coconut sauce

2 tbsp fish sauce

1 tbsp Korean pepper flakes

½ tbsp lime juice

2 tsp fresh ginger, grated

1 tsp liquid smoke

1 tsp chili powder

1 tsp chipotle

1 tsp red pepper flakes

½ tsp cayenne

1 or 2 Thai chilies (optional, to taste)

Himalayan pink salt and pepper, to taste

Chopped green onions and/or grated Parmesan, for garnish

* Any keto-friendly hot sauce will do.

carbs 7g	fibre .5g	fat 61g	protein 75g

This is a big favourite of Hubby's. In Geoff's pre-keto days, General Tso's Chicken Wings were always his favourite at a Chinese restaurant. Nowadays we don't eat out a lot, and when we do, Chinese food isn't high on the list; there are just too many surprise ingredients in there for our liking.

I worked my way through this recipe while Geoff was at work, as I wanted it to be a surprise. I told him I was making wings, but just let him believe they were regular old wings with hot sauce. I served them as a late-night snack for us both. The lights were low so he couldn't tell the difference until his first bite. Boy, was he ever surprised! His eyes lit up like a Christmas tree! Good thing I made an extra big batch that night because they got gobbled up very quickly.

This is a great snack to serve your guests or your family. You can even serve this one to your biggest keto critics and they will never know they're eating "diet" food.

GENERAL TSO'S CHICKEN WINGS

SERVINGS 4   **SERVING SIZE** 10 wings

1. Separate wings into flats and drumettes by cutting them at the joint.

2. Spread wings in an ovenproof baking dish and cover with sesame oil.

3. Bake at 350°F for 45 minutes or until wings are cooked through and skin is starting to crisp.

4. While wings are baking, combine all ingredients for the sauce in a small saucepan over medium-low heat.

5. Gradually increase heat and whisk until smooth and sauce just starts to boil.

6. Reduce heat and simmer for about 5 minutes. Set aside.

7. Remove the cooked wings from the oven and coat them in sauce using a spoon or brush.

8. Return the wings to the oven and broil at 400°F for about 3-5 minutes, or until sauce starts to bubble and caramelize. Leave the oven door open about an inch when broiling to help the oven reach the desired temperature.

9. Garnish with green onions and/or grated Parmesan.

We discovered halloumi fries in our exploration of the incredible city of London. Tucked away in the west end of Camden Town is the Kerb Market, which combines all of the ultimate foodie's "gotta eat that" destinations in one location. It's one of those places that you want to experience with a handful of your best friends, so you can all select a different dish and share a little taste of each other's food. There are just so many fantastic food options to try there.

One of our favourite dishes there is the delicious halloumi fries featured at Oli Baba. Not only are these fries frikkin' gorgeous to look at, but the taste is out of this world. The pomegranate seeds (arils) combined with the sour-cream sauce and herbs elevate this dish to incredible heights that you and your taste buds will love.

Our Halloumi Cheese Fries have a few tweaks that make them our own. We recommend having them dressed to the nines like we've shown in this recipe, or plain with just salt and pepper. Either way, it's a dish you'll want to do over and over again.

HALLOUMI CHEESE FRIES   SERVINGS 2   SERVING SIZE 4 OZ

1. Deep-fry cheese strips for about 2 minutes, or until outsides are golden brown. Try to keep the fries moving to ensure they crisp on all sides.

2. Transfer to a large bowl and add cumin and chili. Shake the bowl to distribute the spices.

3. Transfer to a serving dish.

4. Combine sour cream and apple cider vinegar. Use a squeeze bottle to drizzle the sour-cream sauce over the fries.

5. Cut the pomegranate in half and use a wooden spoon to tap out the seeds. Add pomegranate rubies to the fries and sprinkle tarragon on top.

FOR THE FRIES

lard, for deep-frying

8 oz halloumi cheese, cut into half-inch strips

1 tsp cumin, toasted

1 tsp ancho chili powder

FOR THE SAUCE

½ cup sour cream

2 tbsp apple cider vinegar

FOR GARNISH

1 pomegranate

1 tsp tarragon

 Serve with Sweet Thai Chili Sauce (page 247) for dipping.

carbs	fibre	fat	protein
1g	0.3g	18g	12g

FOR THE JIGGS' DINNER

salt beef, cut into 2-inch cubes

cabbage, quartered

FOR THE ROAST

extra virgin olive oil

beef or pork roast

Himalayan pink salt and pepper, to taste

1 or 2 cups water

medium onion, diced

3 cloves of garlic, whole

1 carrot, cut into 1-inch squares

FOR THE GRAVY

meat or bacon drippings

broth (beef, chicken, or vegetable)

coconut sauce

cream cheese

xanthan gum (optional)

thyme (a couple of sprigs of fresh or ½ tsp dried)

Himalayan salt and pepper, to taste

FOR THE FRIES

jicama, daikon radish, or turnip, cut into half-inch strips (note: turnip has the highest carbs)

lard

Himalayan salt and pepper, to taste

FOR THE POUTINE

cheese curds

Jiggs' dinner (a.k.a. the traditional boiled dinner) is like mother's milk to most East Coast folks, but that has changed with our keto lifestyle. There are components of Jiggs' dinner that we just can't have without risking our ketosis. So we thought, why not bring that traditional meal into the present? Jiggs' Dinner Poutine combines the salt meat (corned beef), faux potatoes, and gravy from our Sunday dinner, with cheese curds to create a nouveau-cuisine masterpiece. Creamy cheese, crispy fries, salty beef, and scrumptious gravy. Simply divine.

Start by making Jiggs' dinner as you ordinarily would (but without the potatoes, turnip, and carrots). We boil salt beef and cabbage together until done and also usually cook a roast or some other form of meat with gravy.

JIGGS' DINNER POUTINE

FOR THE JIGGS' DINNER

1. Boil the salt beef in a large stockpot.

2. Add quartered cabbage after about 45 minutes and boil until cabbage is soft.

3. Strain and separate the meat from the cabbage. (Broth may be saved for future use.)

FOR THE ROAST

1. Preheat oven to 350°F.

2. Add extra virgin olive oil to the bottom of a heavy roasting pan over medium-high heat on the stovetop.

3. Using a pair of tongs, brown all sides of the roast on the stovetop.

4. Season with Himalayan pink salt and pepper.

5. Add water to the roast to the "shoulders" (i.e., three-quarters of the way up the roast, leaving the top of the meat out of the water).

6. Cover and roast in the oven for about 45 minutes.

7. Remove roast from the oven and add the onion, garlic, and carrot.

CONTINUES ▶

8. Check to see if you need to top up the water at this point.

9. Return to the oven for another hour or until the roast reaches the desired doneness.

10. Remove from the oven. Remove the roast from the roasting pan and let rest.

11. Reserve drippings in the pan.

FOR THE GRAVY

1. Transfer the roasting pan to the stovetop over medium heat.

2. Use broth to deglaze pan and get all those tasty bits off the bottom. A serving spoon can be used to scrape the bottom of the pan.

3. Use a masher to incorporate all the bits of garlic and carrot into the broth. Remove any unwanted pieces with a slotted spoon.

4. Keep heat at a simmer.

5. Add coconut sauce and cream cheese and whisk until smooth.

6. Slowly add in xanthan gum, if using, keeping in mind that the xanthan gum will thicken more as it cools.

7. Add thyme, salt, and pepper.

FOR THE FRIES

1. Blanch vegetable strips in a pot of boiling water for at least 10 minutes and then dry completely on a paper towel.

2. Add strips to deep-fryer and cook at 350°F until the outsides are crisp and the inside is soft and warm.

3. Remove to a bowl and toss in salt and pepper.

PUTTING IT ALL TOGETHER

1. Pile the fries high on a plate with the roasted meat and cabbage on the side.

2. Place the salt beef and cheese curds throughout the piled fries.

3. Cover the dressed fries with gravy and enjoy!

Gravy measurements are left vague on purpose. The amounts will vary greatly depending on the amount of drippings you have.

We spice our fries up with garlic and chili powder for added flavour.

Due to the wide variances in each component of this complex dish, we recommend you work out your own macros for this recipe.

I wasn't always a fan of Mom's egg salad. In my earlier years, before my palate developed and when my tastes were limited, I just couldn't get past the egg smell.

When I finally did, I was in love. I quickly found out that Mom's ultimate egg salad was a step above most out there. I don't know if it is the added cottage cheese or the chopped texture that adds something to the equation, but I know I sampled many others that didn't come close to Mom's special blend.

MOM'S ULTIMATE EGG SALAD UNWICH

SERVINGS 2   **SERVING SIZE** 1 unwich

1. Mix all ingredients in a small bowl until blended.

2. Serve on a lettuce leaf or spoon it up.

2   hard-boiled eggs, cut into rough chunks

¼   cup cottage cheese or crème fraîche

2   tbsp Keto Mayonnaise (page 227)

1   tsp apple cider vinegar

½   tsp Newfoundland (a.k.a. summer) savoury

½   tsp onion powder

Himalayan salt and pepper, to taste

chopped chives, to garnish

 If you don't have any Newfoundland savoury, thyme is a close second.

carbs	fibre	fat	protein
1.5g	.5g	15.5g	9.5g

This is a super easy dish that gives you full flavour and will keep your guests occupied while you put the finishing touches on the main course. Make sure you serve the mussels in their shells. Part of the decadence of this dish is the ability to scoop up a little extra white wine sauce with every bite.

2 cups chicken stock or broth

1 cup white wine (Dry is the better keto option.)

½ medium onion, quartered

3 cloves of garlic, finely chopped

4 tbsp fish sauce or 4 sheets seaweed (We use prepackaged seaweed sheets from Costco.)

2 lbs mussels

¼ cup butter, melted

¼ cup fresh dill, chopped

¼ cup fresh thyme, chopped

1 tsp lemon juice

1 tsp red pepper flakes

Himalayan pink salt and pepper, to taste

MUSSELS *in* WHITE WINE AND BUTTER

SERVINGS 4   **SERVING SIZE** ½ pound

1. Combine first 5 ingredients in a stockpot and bring to a boil.

2. Add mussels and reduce heat. Simmer for 5 minutes.

3. Drain liquid with a colander and transfer mussels to a large bowl.

4. Toss mussels with the remaining ingredients and serve.

carbs	fibre	fat	protein
4.75g	.25g	14g	14g

 For extra decadence, add ¼ cup of 35% whipping cream before tossing.

Pumpkin Pie Spice Latte gives you all the flavour of your favourite coffeehouse beverage without all the hidden ingredients. Most commercially purchased pumpkin pie spice mixes are loaded with uglies, and as much as they taste good, they are a keto stall waiting to happen.

The lineup is about to get smaller at the local coffee shop. We've busted through the secret recipe and discovered how to bring this fall favourite into your own home.

PUMPKIN PIE SPICED LATTE

SERVINGS 2   **SERVING SIZE** 1 cup

1. Brew coffee and pour into a large vessel for blending. (We use a Bullet.)

2. Add other ingredients and blend thoroughly. (Use an immersion blender if you don't have a Bullet.)

3. Pour into mugs and top with whipped cream.

2   cups coffee

¼   cup crème fraîche

¼   cup whipping cream (35%)

2   tbsp pumpkin puree

1   tsp confectioner's Swerve (or to taste)

1   tsp vanilla extract

¼   tsp cinnamon

⅛   tsp allspice

⅛   tsp ginger

pinch nutmeg

whipped 35% cream to top

 A cinnamon stick makes a good garnish and pulls double duty as a stir stick.

carbs	fibre	fat	protein
1.5g	.5g	16g	1g

Most gatherings of friends on the East Coast include food, and where there are East Coast food and people, there are usually scallops. More often than not, these are scallops wrapped in bacon. While bacon-wrapped scallops are a great dish for the keto way of eating, we wanted to step outside the box and elevate the dish a little.

Our seared scallops will raise the bar on the hors d'oeuvres for any party. Partridgeberries give this dish a unique East Coast flavour. If you are unable to get your hands on partridgeberries, they can easily be substituted by raspberries or cranberries to get a similar look and flavouring.

SEARED SCALLOPS *with* PARTRIDGEBERRY GASTRIQUE

SERVINGS 4   **SERVING SIZE** ¼ pound

Partridgeberry Gastrique (page 236)

1 lb scallops, patted dry with paper towel

Himalayan pink salt and fresh cracked pepper, to taste

2 tbsp butter

sprig of fresh dill, for garnish

1. Prepare Partridgeberry Gastrique. Set aside.

2. Season scallops on both sides with salt and pepper.

3. Heat a heavy frying pan to high heat and add the butter.

4. Quickly add the scallops and sear at high heat for around 2 minutes then flip them and sear for about 30 seconds on the second side. Make sure not to overcook, which would make the scallops tough and dry.

5. Place the seared scallops on a plate and drizzle the gastrique over top.

6. Garnish with fresh dill and serve.

carbs	fibre	fat	protein
5.75g	1.25g	11.5g	18g

Make sure your scallops are well dried on paper towel before seasoning or they won't brown—and brown means flavour.

Tangy BBQ Buffalo Wings are not only full of healthy fats from the chicken, but they're also deep-fried in healthy lard, giving you twice as much filling flavour! Toss them in our Smokin' BBQ Sauce (page 246), shredded Parmesan cheese, and some fresh herbs, and you've got yourself a great dish. This dish is a triple threat; it can perform as either an appetizer, an amazing late-night snack, or as the star of your main dish.

TANGY BBQ BUFFALO WINGS

SERVINGS 2   **SERVING SIZE** 5 or 6 wings

1. Deep-fry wings at 350°F for about 10 minutes or until crispy.

2. Transfer to a large bowl.

3. Add Smokin' BBQ Sauce and hot sauce, then toss the wings to distribute evenly.

4. Add salt, pepper, and parsley.

5. Plate and sprinkle Parmesan over top.

1 lb chicken wings, flats and drumettes separated

¼ cup Smokin' BBQ Sauce (page 246)

hot sauce, to taste (We use Frank's RedHot.)

¼ cup flat leaf parsley, chopped

Himalayan salt and pepper, to taste

¼ cup Parmesan, grated

carbs	fibre	fat	protein
2.2 g	0 g	46 g	95 g

BREAKFAST & BRUNCH

The timing noted in this recipe will result in a slightly runny egg; adjust if you like your eggs a different consistency.

Want a breakfast that looks like you spent hours in the kitchen, but in reality only took a few minutes to prepare? We've got you covered! This rich and decadent one-pot dish can be finished on your stovetop with a cover, but our preference is to pop it in the oven for the last five minutes of cooking. This recipe will result in a slightly runny egg, increase the cooking time by 30-second increments to find your desired consistency.

Baked Egg Marinara will look like the Cadillac of breakfasts when presented to your overnight guests or family. Only you will know how long it really takes.

½   cup bell peppers, sliced

1   medium tomato, chopped

½   cup spinach, chopped

3   eggs

½   cup Meatless Marinara Sauce (page 232)

Himalayan pink salt and pepper, to taste

¼   cup cheddar, grated

fresh basil, cut into thin strips, for garnish

½   tsp extra virgin olive oil

BAKED EGG MARINARA

SERVINGS 3   **SERVING SIZE** 1 egg + ⅓ of the sauce

1.   Sauté the bell peppers for 3-5 minutes in a medium oven-safe pan over medium heat.

2.   Add tomato and spinach to the pan and then immediately add ½ cup of Meatless Marinara Sauce. Sauce should just cover the bottom of the pan.

3.   Crack your eggs directly into the marinara sauce and add salt and pepper to taste.

4.   Cover and place the pan in a 350°F oven for the final 5 minutes, or simply leave it on your stovetop for the same amount of time.

5.   Remove cover and garnish with cheese, basil, and extra virgin olive oil.

carbs 3.8g	fibre .8g	fat 9g	protein 6.7g

Serve this dish family style and place the pan on a trivet at your dining table for a steaming presentation.

Some mornings you just want to throw it all in a pan, twitch your nose (à la *Bewitched*), and presto, your meal is made. Unless you have a personal chef, or a spouse that's kind enough to do it for you, this recipe is as close as you can get.

A great frittata is a dish you can have for breakfast, lunch, or supper. You can change it up and add any combination of meats and veggies and create your own flavour profile. This just happens to be what our family prefers in our *East Coast Keto* kitchen.

BREAKFAST FRITTATA

SERVINGS 4   **SERVING SIZE** 1 slice

1. Preheat oven to 350°F.
2. Combine eggs, salt, pepper, spices, cheese, and white portion of green onion in a bowl.
3. Melt butter/fat in an ovenproof sauté pan.
4. Add peppers to pan and sauté for 1 minute.
5. Add tomatoes and bacon to pan and turn off heat.
6. Add egg mixture to sauté pan.
7. Transfer to oven and bake for 10 minutes.
8. Remove from oven and sprinkle green onion tops and grated cheddar on top.
9. Bake for another 5 minutes or until cooked.

8   eggs, scrambled

Himalayan salt and pepper, to taste

⅛   tsp thyme

⅛   tsp cumin

⅓   cup cheese, grated (We used Gruyère.)

1   stalk green onion, chopped (Separate the green and white portions.)

2   tbsp butter or bacon fat

½   cup bell peppers, sliced into strips

⅓   cup cherry tomatoes, halved and dried/drained on a paper towel

6   strips of precooked bacon, chopped

¼   cup cheese grated, to top (We used old cheddar.)

 Bake time depends on the size and depth of your pan.

Do not overcook. Frittata should be slightly jiggly in the centre.

Other spices can be substituted.

carbs	fibre	fat	protein
2.5g	.5g	41g	24g

Whether we brew it at home or pick it up at the closest drive-thru window, most of us are more than used to waking up in the morning and starting our day with a cup of joe. You're not really awake until you feel that coffee rush. It can take as few as ten minutes from drinking coffee for caffeine to enter your bloodstream. From there it all happens fairly quickly—caffeine stimulates the release of adrenalin, which gives us that big burst of energy and attentiveness associated with a morning coffee.

But that caffeine burst only lasts a short time. Wouldn't it be great if you could drink that coffee and have the effect last throughout the day? Bulletproof Coffee does exactly that!

The most basic form of Bulletproof Coffee (BPC) is coffee blended up with healthy fats to create a thick, foamy, frothy drink. BPC boasts many benefits, from improved mood, increased energy and memory, faster weight loss, and improved brain power. Instead of fizzling out on you midway through the day like regular coffee, the healthy fats in BPC team up with the caffeine, bringing you increased energy throughout the day, as well as keeping your tummy feeling full. Most ketonians use BPC as a meal replacement. It's a great fix for those who want to consume healthy fats to start their day but don't have the time or the stomach to eat a big meal of eggs and bacon.

But we recommend you use this tool sparingly. While it's a delicious way to get extra fats in, having one or two BPCs daily can catch up to you and result in too much fat consumption. (While keto is generally a higher fat diet, we should use the fats to satisfy our hunger and shouldn't feel the need to consume our macros on a daily basis.)

BULLETPROOF COFFEE

SERVINGS 1   **SERVING SIZE** 1½ cups

1. Blend all ingredients thoroughly in a blender or Bullet and enjoy.

Blending thoroughly is what transforms oily, greasy coffee into the foamiest, frothiest, and smoothest cup of coffee you've ever had.

1½   cups coffee (or alternative)

2   tbsp unsalted butter (Grass-fed is ideal but not necessary.)

2   tbsp coconut oil (or 1 tbsp MCT oil)

1   tbsp 35% whipping cream (optional)

1   tsp vanilla extract (optional)

1   packet stevia or keto-approved sweetener (optional)

carbs	fibre	fat	protein
0g	0g	58g	0g

For those who don't drink coffee, you can also "bulletproof" matcha, chai tea, hot chocolate, or regular tea.

The traditional Christmas breakfast in the Pike household is an overnight strata; sandwiches made with egg-soaked bread, ham, cheese, mustard, and tomato. They're made the night before and are left to sit in the fridge overnight so the uncooked egg soaks into the bread. Then Christmas morning we take the unbaked sandwiches out of the fridge and put them straight into the oven to cook while we're opening gifts. The aroma makes you want to leave the brightly wrapped packages and head into the kitchen for the real treat.

We fell in love with the Croque Monsieur during a trip to Paris. One bite took us back to Christmas morning and the memory of that tantalizing smell. A traditional Croque Monsieur is a grilled cheese and ham sandwich with a layer of cheese cooked into the outside of the sandwich. It's sinfully good and has an ooey-gooey-yummy factor. This keto version has cheese pancakes instead of bread. It has the same great taste but a fraction of the carbs.

CROQUE MONSIEUR   **SERVINGS** 2   **SERVING SIZE** 1 sandwich

1. Whisk the eggs in a bowl, then add cottage cheese and psyllium husk powder. Set aside.

2. Place a frying pan over low-medium heat. Add butter or oil.

3. Dollop one-quarter of the egg batter onto the pan and cook for 3-5 minutes, flipping once. Repeat to make 4 pancakes.

4. Spread a thin layer of Dijon mustard on one side of two pancakes and top with ham and cheese. Add the second pancakes on top, making two sandwiches.

5. The Croque Monsieur can be eaten at this point, but our preference is to return them to the pan assembled and add another layer of cheese on top. Cover the pan and cook at the lowest setting until cheese is melted.

6. Sprinkle with green onion to finish.

4	eggs
8	oz cottage cheese
1	tbsp ground psyllium husk powder
4	tbsp butter or coconut oil
¼	cup smoked deli ham, thinly sliced
½	cup Swiss, Gruyére, raclette, or mozzarella cheese, shredded
2	tbsp Dijon mustard
1	green onion (tops only), minced

 Mustard can be omitted or increased according to your taste, but note the mustard makes this dish. Try it first with it included.

 Top with an over easy egg for a Croque Madame.

carbs	fibre	fat	protein
8.5g	2g	26g	43.5g

We find it takes two to get the perfect timing of this Easy Eggs Benny recipe, one to make the sauce and one to poach the eggs. If the sauce is made before the eggs are ready, set it where it will keep warm.

Butter must be added slowly (tempered) for the hollandaise sauce or the eggs will scramble.

Some people crack the eggs directly into the boiling water, but we've found that cracking them in a bowl instead is a tried and true method for perfect poached eggs. It also makes all the difference to stir the water so that it is moving in a circular motion when you drop in the egg from the bowl.

4   large eggs

4   thick slices of cooked ham or 8 slices of bacon, cooked to your liking

FOR THE HOLLANDAISE

4   large egg yolks

1   tbsp lemon juice

½   tsp Himalayan pink salt

dash of cayenne or Tabasco

⅔   cup hot melted butter

FOR GARNISH

¼   tsp paprika

1   tsp chopped chives (optional)

carbs 3.8g	fibre .8g	fat 9g	protein 6.7g

One of the secrets to the perfect eggs Benedict is the hollandaise sauce. Hollandaise is known as one of the "mother sauces" in classic French cuisine, and although many home cooks are intimidated by it, hollandaise is really quite simple. While we prefer to use an immersion blender, a conventional blender could be used instead, as could just a plain whisk in a bowl.

The timing of this dish does require some careful orchestration; it might take a little practice to get it perfect. We find tag-teaming between the two of us makes for an Easy Eggs Benny. As a base for the poached eggs, we prefer to simply use a thick slice of cooked ham, topped with a couple of slices of bacon.

EASY EGGS BENNY

SERVINGS 3   **SERVING SIZE** 1 egg

1.   Prepare the ham and bacon to your liking.

2.   Bring a pot of water to a rolling boil.

3.   While waiting for the water to boil, crack your eggs into a bowl so they're ready to drop in, and dress plates with a slice of ham topped with some bacon.

4.   Using a slotted spoon, stir the water to create a circular motion in the pot and then drop the eggs into the hot water, one at a time, taking care to keep the water moving as you do so. For a runny yolk (our favourite), the egg will be ready in about 2 minutes. Increase cooking time by increments of 30 seconds for firmer yolks.

5.   Use a slotted spoon to lift each egg from the water.

6.   Place the egg on top of the ham/bacon.

FOR THE HOLLANDAISE

1.   Add the egg yolks, lemon juice, salt, and cayenne to your blender and blend at a medium speed for 20 to 30 seconds.

2.   Slowly add the hot butter to the egg yolk mixture as you continue to blend at a low speed.

3.   Pour the warm hollandaise over the top of the egg and sprinkle paprika on top. Top with fresh chives, if using.

If you prefer, any keto-friendly bun can be used as an addition to the base as you build up your dish.

This is the keto pancake recipe that you've been looking for! Betcha they taste just like the ones your mom made from scratch, if not better.

The secret to getting Light and Fluffy Keto Pancakes just right is to toggle the heat on the stove. You want the heat a little higher just as the batter hits the pan, so the edges form properly and the batter doesn't spread. Then you turn the heat back to low and give the insides of the pancake a chance to cook without burning the bottom.

This recipe yields four pancakes. Increase ingredients incrementally for larger servings. And be sure to have our Buttery and Rich Pancake Syrup (page 208) on hand before you start cooking them!

LIGHT AND FLUFFY KETO PANCAKES

SERVINGS 2   **SERVING SIZE** 2 pancakes

1. Combine all ingredients in a bowl and whisk until they form a thick batter.

2. Heat coconut oil in a sauté or frying pan over medium heat.

3. Spoon 2 tbsp batter into the pan for each pancake.

4. Reduce heat to low to allow the centre of the pancake to cook slowly.

5. Turn the pancake after about 2 minutes, or when the bottom is a golden brown.

6. Cook for about 1 minute on the other side. Plate the pancake and serve hot with our Buttery and Rich Pancake Syrup.

coconut oil, for frying

3   eggs

3   tbsp crème fraîche, heaping

1   tbsp psyllium husk

1   tbsp coconut flour

⅛   tsp cream of tartar

Recipe can be made in a waffle maker as well. It can also be converted into crepes. Just keep the heat down and let the batter spread over the entire pan.

carbs	fibre	fat	protein
4.5g	3g	16.5g	10.5g

This recipe is for the casserole version. If you are baking the eggs in the avocado halves, do not scoop out the whole fruit—just enough for the egg to fit. Layer the ingredients in the same order right in the avocado half.

Avocado baked egg is one of our most delectable and decadent breakfasts. There is no taste quite like creamy avocado with a perfectly cooked egg. Usually, we prepare it as a casserole, but when we have guests for brunch, we usually jazz it up a little and cook it right in the avocado skins. It's hard to top Mother Nature's own presentation. In this case, scoop out some of each avocado half to make room for the egg, then place each avocado half in a ramekin and cook them individually. We like the yolks nice and runny, so we separate the yolk from the whites. We precook the whites, then add the yolks at the last minute to warm them into a yummy goodness.

MEXICAN AVOCADO EGG BAKE

SERVINGS 2   **SERVING SIZE** 2 eggs

1. Preheat oven to 400°F.
2. Cut the avocados in half and remove the pits.
3. Scoop out the avocado by running a spoon just under the skin.
4. Slice avocado lengthwise into quarters and place the slices in a single layer in a small casserole dish.
5. Sprinkle cumin and chili powder over the top of the avocado and spray with olive oil. (We use a refillable oil aerator, found at most department stores.)
6. Crack one egg at a time and separate the egg whites from the yolks, setting the yolks aside.
7. Pour the egg whites over the sliced avocado and top with crumbled bacon.
8. Add Himalayan salt and pepper to taste.
9. Bake for 12 minutes.
10. Remove from the oven and add egg yolks, strategically placing them over the top of the avocado egg white mix.
11. Top with shredded cheese.
12. Return to the oven and bake for 7 minutes.

2   avocados

½   tsp cumin

½   tsp chili powder

olive oil

4   eggs

crumbled bacon

Himalayan salt and pepper, to taste

½   cup shredded cheddar cheese, to finish

carbs	fibre	fat	protein
13.5g	10.5g	55g	18.5g

 We serve this dish with our favourite hot sauce or salsa.

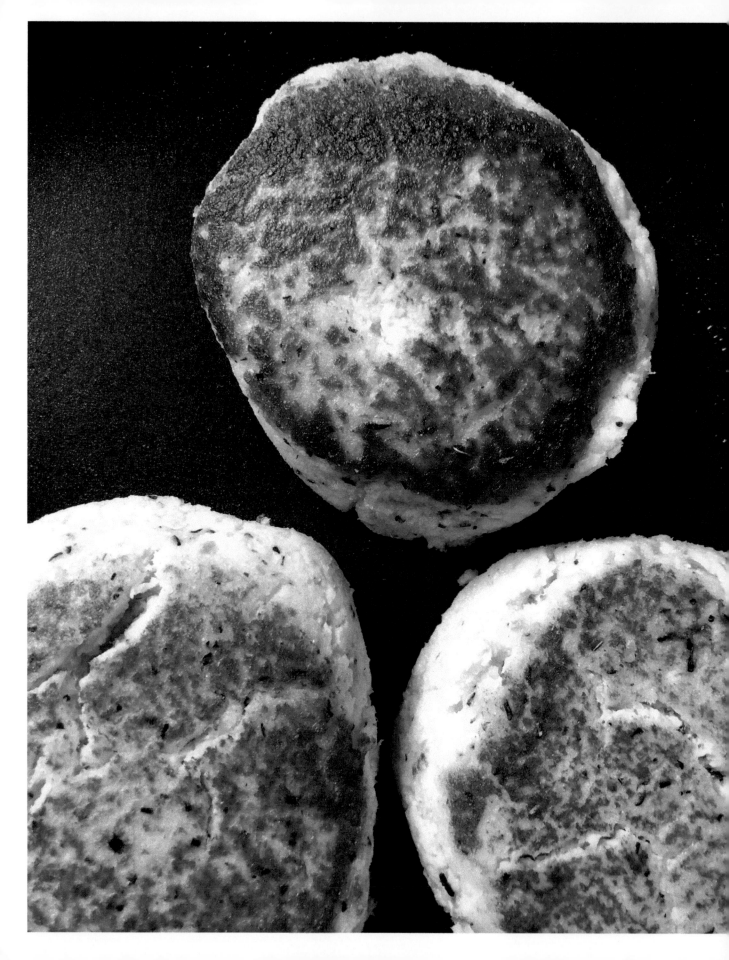

Fish cakes were a staple for most East Coast family dinners or Sunday brunch. Our easy keto fish cakes are made from leftover cod fish, mixed with faux potatoes (i.e., cauliflower), onion, and spices. These Newfoundland Fish Cakes are so close to the real thing that they are good enough to fool even your grandmother.

Since you've been enjoying the keto lifestyle and that slim waist, I'm willing to bet you thought you would never get to taste another Newfoundland fish cake again. It took us a while to find the right ratio of cauliflower to fish for fish cakes that satisfied our own taste. The first couple of versions were either too fishy or too full of cauliflower. We suggest that you give our version a try and then feel free to tweak the recipe to your own tastes.

Newfoundland Fish Cakes have to be made with cod, of course. Add some of our Perfectly Pickled Chanterelles (page 239) and you're all set for a delicious family meal.

Newfoundland Fish Cakes are a perfect replacement for the home-cooked meal that your parents made, but with some small keto substitutes. With these fish cakes, you can safely indulge and be confident that your low carb or keto macros are fine and you don't have to fear the scales.

NEWFOUNDLAND FISH CAKES

SERVINGS 4   **SERVING SIZE** 1 fish cake

1. Boil the cauliflower rice, then set it on paper towels and squeeze to remove excess water.

2. Boil fish until it flakes easily.

3. Blend cauliflower and fish in a Bullet or blender. Set aside.

4. Melt the butter in a frying pan over medium heat and sauté the onion until translucent.

5. Add the garlic and cook for an additional 2 minutes.

6. Season with salt and pepper and set aside to cool slightly.

7. Combine all ingredients in a large bowl and assemble into cakes.

8. Cook in the buttered frying pan over medium heat for 3-5 minutes on each side.

Make certain to squeeze all the water out of the cauliflower for a good consistency.

Don't overfill the pan. Add more butter to the pan as needed.

Try this recipe with keto-friendly corned beef instead of fish.

1 cup cauliflower rice

1 lb boneless cod, skinned

4 tbsp butter

medium onion, diced

3 cloves of garlic, minced

1 tsp Himalayan pink salt

½ tsp black pepper

2 tbsp Newfoundland (a.k.a. summer) savoury or parsley

1 handful chives, chopped

2 large eggs

4 tbsp almond flour

Cauliflower rice is cauliflower that has been finely chopped to resemble a rice texture. We use a food processor to reach our desired texture.

carbs	fibre	fat	protein
6.5g	2.75g	18g	26g

Cake for breakfast is unthinkable, right? How about keto-approved Red Velvet Pancakes with Cream Cheese Sauce? Sign me up! These are great for breakfast—and dessert. I guess, really, they're good for any old time of day. The recipe for Cream Cheese Sauce is on page 216.

We recommend that you keep these on the small side, especially to start, as they can be challenging to flip. We also notice that the amount of food colouring will change with the brand, so experiment until you get the colour you want.

RED VELVET PANCAKES

SERVINGS 6   **SERVING SIZE** 2 pancakes

1	tbsp unsweetened cocoa powder
½	cup coconut flour
½	cup almond flour
2	tbsp Swerve (or other low-carb sweetener)
1	tsp cream of tartar
½	tsp baking soda
½	tsp Himalayan pink salt
4	eggs
1	cup coconut milk
1	tsp vanilla extract
1½	tsp red food colouring
2	tbsp butter

1. Combine dry ingredients.
2. In a large bowl, whisk the eggs until frothy.
3. Add coconut milk to eggs. Beat well.
4. Add remaining ingredients and mix into a batter.
5. Melt the butter in a frying pan on medium heat.
6. Add small amounts of batter into pan and cook over medium heat for about 3 minutes. Lots of bubbles will appear when the pancake is ready to flip. Flip the pancake and cook on the other side for 2-3 minutes, or until the pancake is cooked through.

carbs	fibre	fat	protein
8g	5g	13g	8g

 Amount of cocoa and food colouring may be adjusted to your own taste.

I remember going out for brunch with my parents when I was a small girl. We often went out for supper, but rarely did for the meals earlier in the day. So brunch out as a family was a real treat. We kids would usually opt for pancakes and waffles with maybe bacon or sausage on the side. Mom would have coffee, toast, and scrambled eggs, and Dad always has the western sandwich. I can remember as plain as day watching Dad eat his meal with obvious joy. At the end, he literally licked every finger, savouring every morsel. As a kid, I was content with my sugary meal and I never understood the appeal.

I finally discovered joys of the western sandwich at the end of a week-long family holiday. This time I was the mom, and Hubby, son, and I were travelling across the province, on our way home. We had just broken camp and it had taken far longer than we expected. Our hopes of having a breakfast along the way were pretty bleak. It was too late in the morning. We stopped at a Big Stop on the highway and found ourselves a table. Menus were passed around and we all had a look, trying to decide what we would have for our meal, now almost lunch time. It was then that I saw it and remembered. Western sandwich! The perfect way to enjoy breakfast after breakfast hours. I was officially hooked.

This keto version of the western has no bread. It can be served on a bed of lettuce or other low-carb, keto option. We prefer to have it on the bare plate, topped with grated cheese and our Keto Mayonnaise (page 227). Keto-friendly, keto easy.

WESTERN UNWICH

SERVINGS 2   **SERVING SIZE** 3 eggs

1. Whisk the eggs, salt, pepper, and whipping cream together until well blended.

2. Melt the butter in a medium-sized pan over medium heat.

3. Sauté the onion until translucent.

4. Add peppers and continue to cook for about 3 minutes, until soft.

5. Add precooked bacon/ham just before adding the egg mixture.

6. Reduce heat to low-medium and pour the egg mixture into the pan.

7. Cook the eggs, stirring constantly. The secret is to keep them moving. The final product should be moist and creamy. Don't overcook. They will continue to cook after you plate them.

8. Divide the egg mixture into serving sized portions and plate, topping with a dollop of mayo and a sprinkle of grated cheese.

If you like things on the spicy side, add a few drops of hot sauce to the egg mixture. Or you can add a dash or two to the top of the plated dish.

In season, add 2-3 tablespoons of finely chopped chives to the egg mixture about 15 seconds before you take it from the pan.

6   large eggs

Himalayan salt and pepper, to taste

½   cup whipping cream (35%)

2   tbsp butter

⅓   cup onion, chopped

¼   cup peppers, finely chopped

¾   cup cooked ham or bacon, chopped (Our preference is bacon; it's better to help maintain those electrolytes.)

½   cup old cheddar cheese, grated

4   tbsp Keto Mayonnaise (page 227)

carbs	fibre	fat	protein
7g	1g	70g	45g

Wicked Homemade Waffles will get the crowd out of bed faster than any other breakfast. These light and fluffy Belgian-style keto waffles make a meal all on their own but also do well served alongside bacon or sausages. We serve ours with whipped cream and bakeapples, a Newfoundland treat and member of the raspberry family that grows low to the ground in bogs and marshes, known outside of Atlantic Canada as cloudberries.

Dress up Wicked Homemade Waffles by throwing a handful of blueberries into the batter, or serve them alongside a piece of our Best-Ever Breaded Chicken (page 148) for an extra special treat. Wicked Homemade Waffles are an indulgent yet healthy breakfast for you and your family.

WICKED HOMEMADE WAFFLES

SERVINGS 4 **SERVING SIZE** 1 waffle

2	large eggs
½	cup almond flour
¼	cup coconut flour
3	tbsp confectioner's Swerve
1	tbsp psyllium husk, ground
1½	tsp cream of tartar
1	tsp baking soda
1	tsp xanthan gum
¼	teaspoon Himalayan pink salt
½	cup water
½	cup crème fraîche
¼	cup coconut oil
1	tsp vanilla extract

1. Separate the eggs and set the yolks aside for later in the recipe.

2. Beat the whites with an electric mixer until stiff peaks form, then set aside.

3. Combine all dry ingredients with a whisk.

4. Create a well in the centre of the dry ingredients and add remaining ingredients, except egg whites. Combine well.

5. Gently fold in egg whites with a spatula.

6. Pour waffle mix into a waffle iron set at medium-high.

7. After about 1 minute, turn the heat on waffle iron down slightly to allow the insides of the waffle to cook.

8. Serve with your favourite topping.

carbs	fibre	fat	protein
8.75g	4g	36g	8g

Waffle mixture will expand as it heats, so don't overload your waffle iron.

Turn your waffle iron over and open it upside down to allow each side of the cooked waffle to fall out of the waffle form.

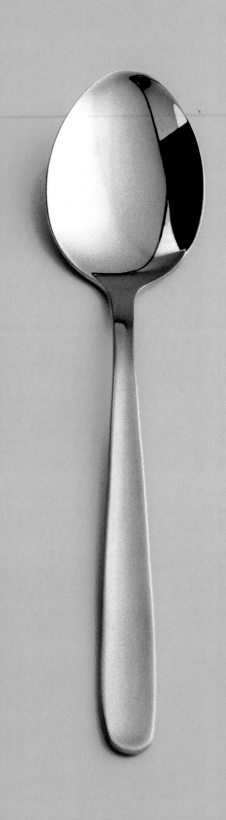

SOUPS & STEWS

Creating and building an Asian flavour is part of the fun of this dish, but that's nothing compared to getting face and eyes into this bowl of Vietnamese delight. Traditionally topped with bean sprouts, mint, Thai basil sprigs, and fresh cilantro leaves, our version has wilted spinach leaves and a soft-boiled egg and green onions for garnish.

BEEF AND GINGER PHO

SERVINGS 2   **SERVING SIZE** 1 large bowl

2 tbsp sesame oil

1 medium onion, finely diced

2 cloves of garlic, finely diced

8 oz beef or stew meat, sliced into long strips (We prefer flank steak.)

1 tbsp red pepper flakes

1 tsp cumin

1 tsp coriander

1 tsp garam masala

1 tsp thyme

1 tsp turmeric

Himalayan salt and pepper, to taste

1 tbsp fish sauce (optional)

1 cup baby spinach

1 tbsp fresh ginger, grated

2 eggs

4 cups beef broth

hot sauce

1 package of shirataki or konjac noodles (We use NuPasta angel hair, 250 g, rinsed well and drained.)

green onion, chopped, for garnish

1. In a deep sauté pan over medium heat, add the sesame oil.

2. Add onion and sauté until translucent. Lower heat to a simmer.

3. Add garlic and beef and cook for 5 minutes. Then turn beef over and continue to cook for another 2 minutes.

4. Push onion, garlic, and beef to the sides of the pan and add the spices, salt, and pepper, directly onto the oil in the centre of the pan. This allows the flavours to bloom and intensify. Cook for 1 minute, then combine the oiled spices with the onion, garlic, and beef.

5. Remove beef mixture from the pan and set aside.

6. Add fish sauce, spinach, and grated ginger. Simmer for 3 minutes.

7. In the meantime, set eggs into cold water in a small saucepan. Bring to a boil and boil for 3-4 minutes, not longer. Remove from heat and immerse in cool water to stop the eggs from cooking.

8. Add beef broth, hot sauce, and noodles to the pan and simmer on low heat for 10 minutes.

9. Chop the beef. (If using flank steak, make sure you chop against the grain.)

10. Peel the eggs and cut them in half lengthwise.

11. Spoon noodles and broth into bowls and arrange beef and eggs on top of the noodles.* (You'll have to separate the beef, which is usually together in one mass.) Sprinkle with green onion to garnish, then serve.

carbs	fibre	fat	protein
5g	2g	31g	28g

 The individual components of the soup are usually arranged together in piles for presentation but can just be all mixed together.

You can use any type of bones for this luxurious broth, with or without the meat. Any skin, gristle, and/or fat can also be added to increase the richness of the broth. Roasting your bones and veggies in advance brings extra depth of flavour to the whole pot, and simmering the broth for an extended period of time allows the collagen in the bones to be released, forming a gelatin. The vinegar helps to extract the collagen and other goodness from the bones to make sure you get the most out of your broth.

Bone broth is rich in amino acids and antioxidants. Drinking this bone broth is a perfect way to keep your electrolytes where they should be and also stay satisfied during the cold winter months. There is nothing as soothing on a cold winter's day. I normally sip it straight out of a mug, but it can also be used for recipes that call for broth.

If using a pressure cooker, lock the lid and set to high for 120 minutes with a natural pressure release.

If using a Dutch oven or slow cooker, cover with a lid and cook for 10-48 hours.

The longer you cook the broth, the more collagen and nutrients you will extract.

BONE BROTH   SERVINGS 8   SERVING SIZE 1 cup

1. Roast the bones in a baking dish for 1 hour at 400°F.
2. Arrange the carrots, celery, onion, and garlic on a large baking sheet in a single layer and drizzle the olive oil over the vegetables.
3. Roast the vegetables in the preheated oven, turning every 20 minutes, until tender and browned, about 1 hour.
4. Transfer the bones, veggies, and all other ingredients into a large stockpot, making sure all ingredients are completely covered with water, and bring to a boil.
5. Reduce heat to low and let simmer for 12-24 hours.
6. Add water as needed to keep all the ingredients submerged.
7. When the broth is a dark, rich brown, remove from heat.
8. Use a slotted spoon to removes the bones.
9. Strain vegetables through a wire strainer or cheesecloth, squeezing out all liquid before discarding.
10. Cool to room temperature, then pour into jars and let cool.
11. When ready to serve, heat to the desired temperature in individual portions. The gel will turn into a liquid again when it is heated.

4	lbs of bones (large chicken bones, marrow bones, beef bones)
2	medium carrots, quartered
2	medium celery stalks, cut into 2-inch pieces
1	medium white onion, quartered with skin on
1	head of garlic, with top cut off and skin on
2-3	tbsp extra virgin olive oil
4	Roma tomatoes
½	cup apple cider vinegar
2	tbsp Himalayan pink salt
1	tsp fresh cracked pepper
2	bay leaves

bundle of herbs (We use 2 sprigs of thyme and 1 sprig each of chamomile and rosemary.)

8-10 cups water

This broth is quite thick and rich. We add a little extra water to our mug to reach desired flavour.

carbs	fibre	fat	protein
6g	1.5g	6g	2g

Unstuffed Cabbage Rolls is a crowd-pleasing, quick and easy, family favourite meal. It's an all-in-one dish with full robust taste in every spoonful.

I can still remember the smells coming from the kitchen, with Mom in her apron, pretty as a picture and busy as a bee. Cabbage rolls were an all-day affair, parboiling the leaves to make them soft enough to roll around the filling, preparing the rice and meat, and then finally combining all the ingredients into little stuffed bundles of culinary joy. By the time she got the meal ready and on the table, she was probably too tired to fully enjoy her creation.

Cabbage Soup [Unstuffed Cabbage Rolls] is the perfect warm-up for a cool fall day. It has all the ingredients and all the rich tomato flavour of a big pot of cabbage rolls, without any of the fuss.

2   tbsp bacon fat or extra virgin olive oil

½   medium onion, chopped

1   lb ground beef

3   cloves of garlic, minced

1   tsp oregano

3   tbsp fish sauce

2   tbsp coconut sauce

1   head cabbage, sliced into strips

1   can (28 oz) diced tomatoes and juice

6   cups chicken broth

Himalayan pink salt and pepper, to taste

CABBAGE SOUP [A.K.A. UNSTUFFED CABBAGE ROLLS]

SERVINGS 8   **SERVING SIZE** 1 bowl

1. Preheat a large pot over medium heat.

2. Add bacon fat or extra virgin olive oil.

3. Add onion and cook for 5 minutes, until translucent.

4. Add ground beef and brown for 5-7 minutes.

5. Push meat and onion to the sides of the pot and add garlic, oregano, and fish and coconut sauces.

6. Stir in cabbage and cook for 10 minutes, adding water if needed to keep the cabbage from burning.

7. Reduce heat to a simmer and stir in tomatoes and chicken broth.

8. Season with salt and pepper to taste.

9. Cover and cook on medium-low for about 30 minutes or until cabbage is soft.

carbs	fibre	fat	protein
11g	4g	29g	16g

When you're not feeling your best, there's nothing like a bowl of chicken noodle soup to make you feel better. A warm, aromatic serving of chicken noodle soup is, for most people, the food equivalent to a bowl of compassion and love.

Over the years, our chicken noodle soup (with non-keto ingredients) helped us through many a sniffle in our home. We knew we had to figure out a keto alternate so we would be prepared for when those days hit.

Chayote squash in its raw form looks very similar to a green apple that has been squashed or crumpled on one side. Once cut, seeded, and peeled, chayote tastes very much like a cross between a potato and an apple. When cooked up in a soup or stew, chayote makes a great replacement for potato.

For the noodles, we use the same basic recipe that we use for our Pizza Crust (page 240). We roll it out really thin, then bake the "noodles" for half the time you would bake the crust.

These noodles are added into the chicken broth after the soup has been removed from the heat and is just sitting covered. If you add them before this point, they might dissolve into the broth altogether.

You can also use shirataki noodles or any other keto-approved noodles in place of the pizza-crust noodles.

CHICKEN NOODLE SOUP

SERVINGS 4   **SERVING SIZE** 1 bowl

1. Heat the butter or bacon fat in a frying pan over medium heat.
2. Sauté chayote and onion for 10 minutes.
3. Push chayote and onion back to the sides of the pan and add garlic.
4. Reduce heat to low and add spices directly into the oil in the centre of the pan. Allow them to simmer for 5 minutes.
5. Transfer everything to a medium saucepan.
6. Use about ¼ cup of the broth to deglaze the sauté pan. Add remaining chicken broth and chicken to the pot and simmer for 15 minutes.
7. Remove from heat and add noodles.
8. Season with salt and pepper to taste.
9. Cover for 5 minutes and then enjoy.

2	tbsp butter or bacon fat
1	chayote squash, seeded and diced into half-inch pieces
½	onion, diced
2	cloves of garlic, minced
½	tsp marjoram
½	tsp parsley
½	tsp summer savoury
½	tsp thyme
¼	tsp coriander
¼	tsp tarragon
6	cups chicken broth
1½	cups of noodles (adapted as described above from Pizza Crust recipe, page 240)
2	chicken breasts or 4 chicken thighs, precooked and cubed

Himalayan pink salt and pepper, to taste

carbs	fibre	fat	protein
4.25g	1.25g	12g	15.5g

Creamy Chanterelle Mushroom Soup can be made from any mushroom, but the chanterelle adds a distinct nutty or woodsy taste to the dish, not to mention a gorgeous golden colour. Anyone who has done any foraging knows the excitement of discovering a trail of spilled gold hidden on the shadowy forest floor, the air ripe with the distinct apricot or peachy aroma.

This soup can be made with fresh or dried mushrooms, although fresh is always preferred.

CREAMY CHANTERELLE MUSHROOM SOUP

SERVINGS 4   **SERVING SIZE** 1 bowl

1	lb chanterelle mushrooms
3	tbsp butter
½	cup onion, diced
3	cloves of garlic, minced
½	tsp dried thyme leaves
½	tsp Himalayan pink salt
¼	tsp pepper
1	cup dry white wine
4	cups chicken or vegetable broth
½	cup whipping cream (35%)
⅛-¼	tsp xanthan gum
⅛	tsp nutmeg

cream and/or olive oil, to finish

1. Dry fry the mushrooms in a large saucepan until they give up all their water. Remove mushrooms and set aside.

2. Melt butter over medium-high heat.

3. Add the onion and cook until translucent, about 3 minutes.

4. Add garlic, thyme, salt, and pepper.

5. Return mushrooms to the pan, reserving a few for garnish.

6. Add white wine and boil for 3-5 minutes.

7. Add the broth and stir while returning the mixture to a boil.

8. Reduce the heat to medium-low and simmer uncovered, stirring occasionally, for 10 minutes.

9. Remove from heat and let the soup cool slightly. Use an immersion blender to cream the soup.

10. Add whipping cream.

11. Sprinkle in the xanthan gum and nutmeg and simmer on low, whisking constantly for about 30-60 seconds.

12. Finish the soup with a swirl of cream and/or olive oil and a few mushrooms atop each bowl.

carbs	fibre	fat	protein
12.25g	4.75g	20g	7.5g

A ¼ cup of cider vinegar and ½ cup of water can be used instead of the wine.

Egg Drop Soup was our first keto soup. Hubby was feeling a bit under the weather and was jonesing for a cup of chicken noodle. As it was the early keto days, we knew we couldn't have noodles, and our own Chicken Noodle Soup recipe had not yet been born. My creative side went into action and I came up with a killer chicken broth, but it needed a bit of extra substance. Voila, Egg Drop Soup for the sick and weary.

Egg Drop Soup is quick and tasty and will hit all the savoury umami receptors in your tongue. It will also satisfy a 200-pound sick guy and help him survive a bout of man flu.

EGG DROP SOUP   SERVINGS 2   SERVING SIZE 1 bowl

1. Heat sesame oil in a medium sauté pan.

2. Sauté garlic and green onion bulbs until they begin to turn translucent.

3. Add chicken broth, bacon fat (or butter), and ginger. Bring to a boil and stir everything together.

4. Add the chili/pepper flakes and hot sauce. Stir again and simmer for 3 minutes.

5. Season with salt and pepper to taste.

6. Beat the eggs in a separate container. Stir the broth with a spoon to create movement in the pot. Using the tines of a fork, drop the egg into the broth as you continue to move the broth with a spoon. This is a slow process, but it is worth the hassle. Simmer for 2 minutes.

7. Serve in bowls and top with chopped green onion and more hot sauce if desired.

2   tbsp sesame oil

3   cloves of garlic, finely chopped

3   bulbs of green onion, chopped (Reserve the green for garnish.)

1½ cups chicken broth

1   tbsp bacon fat or butter

1   tsp fresh ginger, grated

2   tbsp Korean or red pepper flakes

2   dashes hot sauce

Himalayan pink salt and pepper, to taste

2   large eggs

green onion tops, chopped, for garnish

carbs	fibre	fat	protein
6.5g	1.5g	25g	12.5g

You can make this delicious, tangy recipe your own by choosing your own protein source and adding more or less of the spicy ingredients, but the sour component that defines this soup only happens when you add vinegar. We use apple cider vinegar, but it can be switched out for white vinegar.

This one is Sidekick Geoff's all-time favourite. We make big batches and freeze the extra for quick weekday lunches. An indulgent, spicy taste of home while sitting at your work desk.

HOT AND SOUR SOUP

SERVINGS 6   **SERVING SIZE** 1 bowl

1	tbsp sesame oil
8	oz pork or chicken, thinly sliced
8	oz mushrooms, thinly sliced
¼	cup coconut sauce
8	cups chicken or beef broth
¼	cup apple cider vinegar, or more to taste
1	tbsp hot sauce, or to taste
2	tsp ground ginger
½	tsp xanthan gum
2	large eggs
4	green onions (scallions), thinly sliced

Himalayan salt and pepper, to taste

1. Heat sesame oil in a large stockpot.

2. Add pork or chicken and fry until lightly browned.

3. Add mushrooms and coconut sauce and simmer for 5 minutes.

4. Add broth, vinegar, hot sauce, and ginger to the pot and simmer for 10 minutes.

5. Sprinkle in xanthan gum slowly, keeping in mind that it will thicken as it cools. Easy does it.

6. Whisk the eggs, then drizzle them into the pot in a thin stream while stirring the soup. If you prefer smaller ribbons of egg, whisk the egg as you drizzle it into the soup.

7. Stir in the white part of the green onions/scallions.

8. Add salt and black pepper to taste.

9. Garnish with green onion/scallion tops.

carbs	fibre	fat	protein
5g	2g	31g	28g

 If you'd like a more sour soup, add more vinegar, and if you'd like a spicier soup, add more hot sauce.

The idea for our Moose Bourguignon had its start in a little food market in Camden Town in London where we had a beef bourguignon burger. This was before our low-carb days, and let me tell ya, it was super tasty but oh-so-carb-laden.

We started working on our own version of this dish pretty much as soon as we got home. We used the general idea of that delicious carby sandwich and took it back to its bare-bones roots—the French *boeuf bourguignon*—then swung it back to Newfoundland and chose instead to incorporate our native moose meat. After a few attempts, a star was born!

Our Moose Bourguignon is a meal all on its own, but it can be served with a side salad or grilled veggies.

MOOSE BOURGUIGNON

SERVINGS 6   **SERVING SIZE** 1 bowl

1. Heat bacon fat/butter in a large stockpot or Dutch oven.

2. Add the fat pork and cook over medium heat until pieces of pork are crispy and most of the oil has been rendered out. Remove the pieces of pork (scrunchions) and set aside.

3. Add the moose and cook on the stovetop until brown on all sides. Brown means flavour, so make sure to get it good and brown.

4. Add the carrot, whole pearl onions, wine, and vinegar, covering the meat to the shoulders (i.e., cover three-quarters of the meat, leaving the top quarter uncovered). Adjust liquid as needed.

5. Add the garlic, thyme, salt, and pepper.

6. Bring to a simmer, then cover and place in the oven, adjusting the heat so that the liquid simmers very slowly for 3-4 hours. The meat is done when it easily breaks apart.

7. Pour in the stock, cover, and return to the oven for about 40-50 minutes until the onions and carrot are soft.

8. Remove from the oven and add the mushrooms. Return to the oven for 10 minutes.

9. Sprinkle xanthan gum into the stew and whisk in. Be careful, as it will thicken as it cools.

2	tbsp bacon fat or butter
6	oz salted fat pork (a.k.a. pork fat back)
2	lbs moose meat (or roast beef), cut into 1-inch cubes
1	carrot, peeled and cubed
10-12	white pearl onions
1½	cups red wine
¼	cup apple cider vinegar
3	cloves of garlic, minced
½	tsp thyme
	Himalayan pink salt and pepper, to taste
3	cups beef stock
6	white button mushrooms, sliced
½	tsp xanthan gum

carbs 5.5g	fibre .5g	fat 25g	protein 22.5g

Words cannot express how happy I was to find mung beans.

When you start a keto lifestyle, there are some foods that have to disappear from your diet, but when push comes to shove, it's eye-opening which foods we don't want to part with. Pea soup fit that bill for me. It's not a dish I had often, but for me it's one that resonates with feelings of warmth, comfort, and home. It's a chat after a game of hockey. A warm-up after clearing the driveway of snow. It's sitting down to Nan's table for a homemade scoff.

Mung beans are good to go for keto. The colour is a little different than the traditional split peas, but the taste is just the same. This Newfoundland Mock Split Pea Soup is a little high on the healthy carb-o-meter, but if you're a pea soup fan, you can safely plan it into your day.

NEWFOUNDLAND MOCK SPLIT PEA SOUP

SERVINGS 10   **SERVING SIZE** 1 bowl

1	cup dried mung beans
1	tbsp butter, extra virgin olive oil, or bacon fat
1	medium onion, diced
10	cups water
½-1	lb of salt beef or ham, diced
1	medium turnip, rough chopped
2	carrots, rough chopped

Himalayan pink salt and pepper, to taste

1. Soak mung beans overnight in cold water.

2. Heat butter in a large stockpot over medium-low heat on the stovetop and sauté onions until translucent.

3. Add water, salt beef, and beans and simmer for 30 minutes.

4. Add turnip and carrot, season with salt and pepper, and continue to simmer until veggie pieces are soft and beans have mostly dissolved.

Water can be added after cooking if the soup is too thick.

Diced chayote squash can be added as a potato substitute.

carbs	fibre	fat	protein
15g	5.4g	6.4g	11g

It's impossible to go into an East Coast kitchen that doesn't have its own version of a seafood chowder. Whether its cod, clam, or a mixed variety, you're probably not going to be disappointed with the taste.

Our Seafood Chowder uses a variety of seafood, but you can easily personalize that to suit your own tastes. Serve with Savoury Cheesy Biscuits (page 200) on the side and watch your family and friends devour it and ask for more.

SEAFOOD CHOWDER

SERVINGS 6   **SERVING SIZE** 1 bowl

1. Heat lard/fat in a stockpot.
2. Add chopped onion and sauté until translucent.
3. Add salt beef and garlic and continue to sauté for another 3-5 minutes.
4. Push garlic and onions to the edges of the pot and add spices directly into the oil in the centre and cook for 2 minutes.
5. Add vinegar, fish sauce, and broth. Cover, reduce heat, and cook for about 10 minutes.
6. Add seafood and simmer for 5 minutes or until cooked.
7. Add whipping cream and xanthan gum and simmer for 5-10 minutes.
8. Serve hot.

3	tbsp lard or bacon fat
1	medium onion, chopped
4	oz salt beef
3	cloves of garlic, minced

Himalayan pink salt and pepper to taste

1	tsp thyme
½	tsp Newfoundland (a.k.a. summer) savoury
½	tsp tarragon
2	pinches nutmeg
¼	cup apple cider vinegar
2	tbsp fish sauce
5	cups chicken broth
4	oz scallops, chopped into bite-sized pieces
4	oz salmon, chopped into bite-sized pieces
4	oz shrimp, chopped into bite-sized pieces
12	oz cod, chopped into bite-sized pieces
½	cup whipping cream (35%)
1	tsp xanthan gum

FOR GARNISH

bacon, cooked

green onion, chopped

carbs 3.7g	fibre .7g	fat 18g	protein 24g

FOR THE MEATBALLS

½ lb ground pork

½ lb fresh shrimp, peeled, veined, and roughly chopped (optional)

2 tbsp bacon fat

1 tbsp coconut sauce

1 tbsp grated ginger

1 tsp fish sauce

½ tsp cumin

2 cloves of garlic, minced

2 Thai chilies, finely chopped

Himalayan pink salt and pepper, to taste

1 egg white

FOR THE BROTH

4 cups chicken broth

1 cup bok choy stalks, chopped into 1-inch pieces (Reserve greens.)

1 tbsp coconut sauce

1 tbsp cold-pressed sesame oil

1 tsp fish sauce

¼ tsp red pepper flakes

1-inch piece of ginger, minced

1 lemongrass stalk, smashed and diced

2 cloves of garlic, chopped

Himalayan pink salt and pepper, to taste

green onion, chopped, for garnish

This soup boasts all the bold, rich tastes of the restaurant version without the carby wrappers.

In my pre-keto days, a visit to a Chinese restaurant wasn't complete without a bowl of wonton soup. My love for this soup was so great, at times I chose to indulge in a second bowl as a dessert course.

I don't go into many Chinese restaurants these days, but Chinese home cooking within the keto world is a thing. Unwrapped Wonton Soup is a simple homemade keto fix for everybody's favourite Chinese soup.

UNWRAPPED WONTON SOUP

SERVINGS 4 **SERVING SIZE** 1 bowl

FOR THE MEATBALLS

1. Combine all ingredients into one-inch meatballs and place on a parchment-covered baking sheet. Careful not to overwork the meat, as it will make the meatballs tough.

2. Bake at 350°F for about 20 minutes.

3. Turn the meatballs, then cook for another 5 minutes.

4. Set aside.

FOR THE BROTH

1. Combine broth, white portion of bok choy, coconut sauce, fish sauce, sesame oil, pepper flakes, ginger, lemongrass, garlic, salt, and pepper to a medium stockpot or Dutch oven.

2. Simmer for about 15 minutes, until garlic is soft and tender.

3. Add bok choy greens and simmer for 5 minutes.

4. Spoon broth into bowls and add meatballs.

5. Garnish with green onion.

carbs	fibre	fat	protein
5.6g	.4g	17g	21g

SEAFOOD

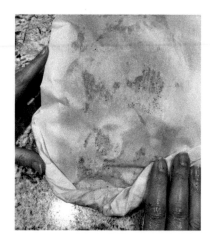

Baking fish in parchment paper is probably one of the most forgiving ways to prepare it. The juices and spices are sealed inside with the fish, so you know the end result will be juicy and tender with lots of taste. We serve these to guests in individual packets. They're like little surprise packages on your plate! You have to open the packets to see what good things are inside.

BAKED COD EN PAPILLOTE

SERVINGS 2

16 oz cod or other white fish

4 tbsp lemon juice or white wine

2 tbsp extra virgin olive oil

½ tsp Korean or red pepper flakes

½ tsp thyme or dill

Himalayan pink salt and pepper, to taste

½ onion, sliced

½ cup bell peppers, sliced into strips

1. Preheat oven to 350°F.

2. Tear off two large sheets of parchment paper, roughly about 20 inches long, and fold in half.

3. Divide the fish into two servings.

4. Open the folded pieces of paper and place the cod pieces in the middle, next to the fold.

5. Drizzle the fish with lemon juice and extra virgin olive oil.

6. Sprinkle the herbs, spices, salt, and pepper directly on top of the fish.

7. Arrange one half of the onion and peppers onto each of the cod pieces.

8. Seal the parchment pieces by folding the parchment in half again and then crimping the edge (see photo) until the packets are completely sealed.

9. Place the sealed packets on a baking sheet and transfer to the oven.

10. Bake until the parchment puffs and the liquid is bubbling, about 20 minutes.

11. Let rest 5 minutes before opening.

carbs	fibre	fat	protein
8g	1.5g	15.5g	41g

Isn't it funny how adding a few extra ingredients can elevate a dish? That's certainly true with a basic cod au gratin. Most of us grew up with fish (in particular cod) on our tables, but for some reason the addition of the cheese, etc., makes this recipe seem all fancy.

We serve this in individual serving dishes when we have guests for dinner. Add a sprig of green parsley for garnish and your guests will think they're dining at a swanky à la carte restaurant.

COD AU GRATIN   SERVINGS 4   SERVING SIZE 1 cup

1. Preheat oven to 375°F.

2. Pat fish pieces dry and cut into bite-sized pieces. (You can leave them as fillets, but we think they incorporate into the dish better cut into chunks.)

3. Place fish pieces into a casserole dish or individual gratin dishes.

4. Meanwhile, heat cheese, butter, and broth in a medium-sized saucepan over low heat until the cheese is melted.

5. Add whipping cream and fish sauce. Simmer to incorporate, about 5 minutes.

6. Add seasonings and xanthan gum.

7. Pour the cheese sauce over the fish in the casserole dish/gratin dishes.

8. Sprinkle pork rinds on top.

9. Place dish(es) in the oven for 30-45 minutes.

10. Remove from oven and let cool for 5 minutes.

4	cups cod fillet
1	cup sharp cheddar cheese, grated
¼	cup Parmesan cheese, grated
3	tbsp butter or bacon fat
1	cup chicken broth
1	cup whipping cream (35%)
2	tsp fish sauce
1	tsp summer savoury or thyme, or to taste
1	tsp Korean pepper flakes or chili powder

Himalayan pink salt and pepper, to taste

1	tsp xanthan gum

pork rinds, crushed

carbs	fibre	fat	protein
3g	0g	38g	48g

Cod and Tomato Bake was a familiar dish from my family's past. Back when I was a kid, I wouldn't try this dish. Like many youngsters I had myself convinced I didn't like fish, but when I finally got around to taking my first bite, I knew I was hooked for life.

Cod and Tomato Bake is a heavenly combination of cod, healthy fats, herbs and spices, and tomato. These ingredients all come together in a rich, savoury dish that will have your family asking for seconds.

COD AND TOMATO BAKE

SERVINGS 4   **SERVING SIZE** 8 oz

1	medium onion, diced
2	cloves of garlic, minced
1	tbsp butter
¼	tsp red pepper flakes
½	tsp basil
½	tsp parsley
½	tsp thyme

Himalayan pink salt and pepper, to taste

2	tbsp extra virgin olive oil
2-2¼	lbs fresh cod fillets
1	can (28 oz) San Marzano tomatoes, chopped into 1-inch pieces
½	cup mozzarella, grated

1. Place onion, garlic, and butter in a microwave-safe dish and microwave for 90 seconds or until onions are translucent.

2. Add pepper flakes and herbs to butter onion mix. Set aside.

3. Preheat oven to 375°F.

4. Cover the bottom of a casserole dish with a thin layer of olive oil.

5. Thoroughly pat dry the cod and place in the casserole dish in a single layer.

6. Spread tomatoes over cod.

7. Spoon onion and herb mix over tomatoes.

8. Transfer to the oven and bake for 30 minutes.

9. Sprinkle mozzarella over the top, then bake for another 5 minutes or until mozzarella is melted.

10. Let cool for 10 minutes before serving.

carbs	fibre	fat	protein
11.75g	2.25g	7g	26g

We pair this with Creamed Spinach (page 186).

Here on the East Coast, deep-fried fish is a thing of beauty that is not to be taken lightly. The success of entire restaurants sometimes rests on the flakiness of the fish and the crunch of the batter.

Of all our recipes, deep-fried fish was one that we wanted to nail right smack dab on the head, and we think we did exactly that. Make sure you keep the batter very loose; it should be more like a wash or a slurry than a traditional fish batter. The coconut flour has a higher absorbency than regular flour, and it should be runnier than you are used to. Depending on what coconut flour you're using, you might have to decrease or increase the suggested amount.

You can either fry the battered fish in oil up to the shoulders or deep-fry. We find that the batter leaves a lot of residue, so we'll only do a batch when we're ready to change the oil in our fryer. Serve this fish with jicama or daikon fries (see the recipe for Jiggs' Dinner Poutine on page 64) and Creamy Keto Coleslaw (page 189).

DEEP-FRIED FISH [AND CHIPS]

SERVINGS 4 **SERVING SIZE** 8 oz

1. Season the individual pieces of cod with salt and pepper on each side. Set aside.

2. Preheat a deep-fryer to 350°F and melt your lard.

3. Combine all the dry ingredients for the batter.

4. Add the egg and soda and whisk.

5. Pat the fish dry with paper towel.

6. Place each piece of fish into the batter and cover thoroughly. We find the batter sticks a little better if you gently massage it into the fish.

7. Drop each piece of fish into hot lard and fry for 3-5 minutes per side, depending on the thickness of your fish.

32 oz cod, cut into 4 pieces

Himalayan salt and pepper, to taste

lard or extra virgin olive oil for deep-frying

FOR THE BATTER

½ cup Parmesan, grated

⅛-¼ cup coconut flour

½ tsp cream of tartar

½ tsp garlic powder

¼ tsp baking soda

Himalayan salt and pepper, to taste

1 egg

1 cup unflavoured club soda

If you prefer, cut the cod into bite-sized pieces first.

You can add any extra spices or herbs you like to the batter.

carbs	fibre	fat	protein
6g	3.25g	19g	49g

Any seafood may be added to the boil, just adjust cooking time in relation to the size of the pieces.

2 cups water

1 cup white wine

½ cup apple cider vinegar

¼ cup Himalayan pink salt

4 sheets seaweed or 4 tbsp fish sauce (We use prepackaged seaweed sheets from Costco.)

2 lemons, cut in half

2 garlic bulbs, cut across the cloves

1 large white onion, quartered

1 tbsp chili flakes

½ tsp pepper

10 to 12 red radishes

4 keto-friendly sausages (i.e., without starches), cut into bite-sized chunks

4 crab clusters (i.e., crab legs with a generous portion of the body attached)

2 lbs mussels

1 lb shrimp, peeled and deveined

4 oz unsalted butter

¼ cup fresh dill, chopped

¼ cup fresh thyme leaves, chopped

We've been lucky to be accepted within the chef world in Newfoundland. As a foodie, there is not a bigger honour than the opportunity to cook with these fine folks.

We've picked up many a culinary tip along the way, from secret ingredients, favourite food/spice combinations, and many how-to tricks of the inner circle. This recipe is one of the ideas we picked up along the way. We've added our own flavour profile and of course made some substitutions to make it keto friendly.

This is a fun hands-on feast for any family/friend gathering. The recipe feeds about three people, but it can be multiplied for a bigger crowd. We hope this dish helps to bring a feeling of contentment to your next family gathering.

EAST COAST SEAFOOD BOIL

SERVINGS 4

1. In a large stockpot, bring water, wine, vinegar, salt, seaweed, lemons, garlic, onion, chili flakes, and pepper to a boil.

2. Lower heat to medium and simmer for 10 minutes.

3. Add radishes and sausage. Continue to simmer for 10 minutes.

4. Add crab, mussels, and shrimp, and cook an additional 5 minutes or until shrimp is pink and mussel shells are open.

5. Strain in a large colander.

6. Transfer to a large bowl.

7. Add butter, dill, and thyme and toss to combine.

8. Empty the contents of the bowl onto a table that has been covered with newspaper and enjoy!

carbs	fibre	fat	protein
7.5g	1.25g	45g	105g

If eating inside, make sure to add a protective insulating layer underneath the newspaper so the heat doesn't ruin your table's finish.

Toss the dish at the table in front of your guests—it adds to the show.

I often wonder what Newfoundland must have looked like to Italian explorer Giovanni Caboto (a.k.a. John Cabot) and his crew when they first spotted our beautiful island. Rumours say that fish (i.e., cod) was so plentiful, they could lower a basket into the Atlantic Ocean and raise it to find the basket teeming with fish. Surely the rivers were full of salmon and trout, and John's crew were well-fed, at least in the summer months.

We were never big salmon fans in our home, but in our opinion the components of this dish all come together to make something extra special that we just love. Thick, rich cream, small cherry tomatoes, and rich aromatic herbs all help to round out this Italian favourite.

With this East Coast Keto version of Tuscan Salmon we tip our hats to John Cabot, the man who "discovered" Newfoundland and Labrador. Our family gobbles it up and almost licks the plates because it's just so good. We hope your people love it too!

JOHN CABOT SALMON

SERVINGS 4   **SERVING SIZE** 2-3 oz

2-4	salmon fillets (2-3 oz per person)
	extra virgin olive oil
	Himalayan pink salt and pepper, to taste
2	cups baby spinach
½	cup cherry tomatoes, halved
½	cup whipping cream (35%)
¼	cup Parmesan, grated
¼	cup salted butter
3	tbsp lemon juice
3	cloves of garlic, minced
½	tsp dry mustard
¼	tsp basil
¼	tsp fennel seed, crushed
¼	tsp parsley
¼	tsp tarragon

1. Heat oven to 400°F. Rub salmon with extra virgin olive oil and season with salt and pepper, then place in ovenproof baking dish.

2. Combine all other ingredients and pour over salmon.

3. Bake for 15 minutes or until salmon flakes with a fork.

carbs	fibre	fat	protein
3.5g	.75g	25g	9g

This restaurant-quality dish is one that can be whipped up in minutes. Creamy and cheesy, rich and decadent, we promise you're going to love it!

SHRIMP ALFREDO

SERVINGS 4   **SERVING SIZE** 6 oz

1	tbsp butter, salted
1	lb raw shrimp, cleaned, with tails on
5	whole sun-dried tomatoes (approx. 1 oz), diced
4	cloves of garlic
4	oz cream cheese
1	tsp dried basil or thyme
1	tsp salt
1	cup whipping cream (35%)
½	cup Parmesan, grated

1. Melt butter in a large sauté pan over medium-low heat.

2. Add the shrimp and cook on each side for about 30 seconds. Don't cook them past this because they will continue to cook when they are added back into the sauce. Overcooking the shrimp will make them tough and rubbery!

3. Remove shrimp and set aside.

4. Add sundried tomatoes and garlic to the pan and cook for 3-5 minutes.

5. Add cream cheese, seasonings, and cream to the pan.

6. Increase the heat to medium. Stir frequently until the cream cheese has melted into the cream and no lumps are present.

7. Add the Parmesan and stir to combine. Let simmer until the sauce begins to thicken.

8. Add shrimp back into the pan and simmer for 5 minutes.

9. Remove from heat and serve by itself or atop konjac noodles.

carbs	fibre	fat	protein
7g	1g	34g	32g

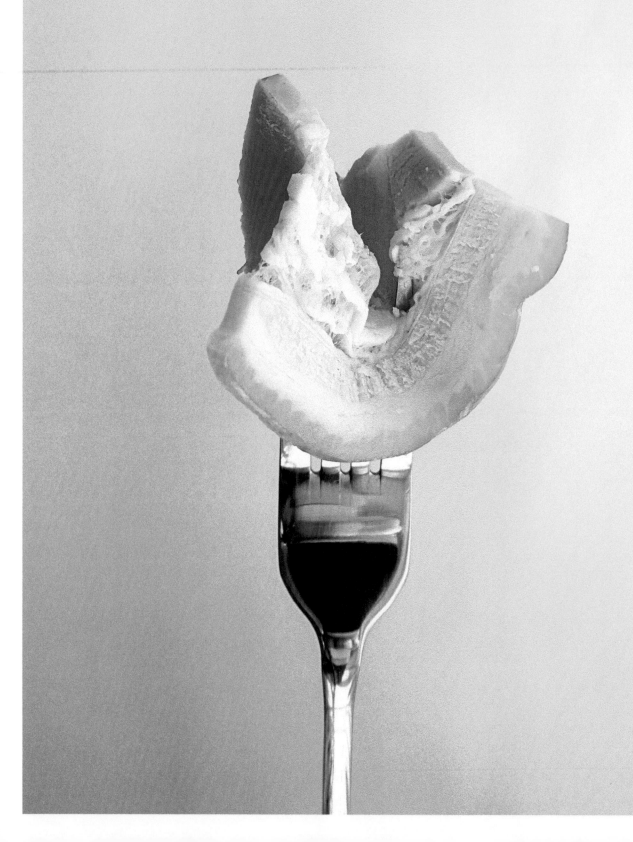

MEAT & POULTRY

FOR THE MEATBALLS

2	lbs ground beef
2	lbs ground pork
6	slices of bacon, ground or finely chopped
4	slices of bacon, diced
2	eggs, lightly beaten
4	oz old cheddar, grated
1	onion, diced
2	cloves of garlic, finely chopped
¼	cup green pepper, finely chopped

vegetables of choice, diced

2	tsp dried oregano
1	tsp parsley
1	tsp basil

Himalayan pink salt and pepper, to taste

FOR THE BACON WEAVE

12 slices of bacon

FOR THE SAUCE

⅛ cup cream cheese

½ tsp xanthan gum

carbs	fibre	fat	protein
2.5g	.5g	47g	29g

Bacon-Covered Meatloaf has become one of our favourite go-to recipes. We have always liked meatloaf, but when a close friend told us about a basic version of this recipe, we knew we had to play with it and make it our own.

The chopped pieces of bacon incorporated in the meatloaf base add to the richness of the dish and almost guarantee that the end product will be juicy and delicious. The added veggies will help you to get some extra goodness into your family's tummies. Add your own veggies of choice (either blended or in bite-sized pieces) and make this meatloaf your own.

BACON-COVERED MEATLOAF

SERVINGS 8   **SERVING SIZE** 1 slice

1. Gently mix all meatloaf ingredients in a large mixing bowl with your hands until thoroughly mixed. (Remember, the more you work the meat, the tougher it will be.)

2. Form the meat mixture into a loaf and set it on a parchment-lined baking tray.

3. Start to make the bacon weave by placing six pieces side by side on a piece of wax paper.

4. Fold every second piece of bacon in half and place another piece of bacon crosswise at the centre of the bed of bacon. Then unfold the folded pieces of bacon back over the crosswise piece. You should now have one piece of bacon woven between the others crosswise in the centre of your weave.

5. Now fold every alternate piece of bacon over (across the piece placed crosswise) and lay down another piece of bacon next to the last one you placed.

6. Repeat the process until you get to the edge, then start on the other side until you have woven six pieces into the original six.

7. Cover the meatloaf with the bacon weave and bake at 350°F for 50 minutes or until thoroughly cooked in the centre.

Values do not include any added veggies.

8. Remove the loaf to a cutting board and gather the drippings in a medium saucepan. Add the cream cheese and xanthan gum and simmer until the cream cheese has melted and the drippings are fully incorporated. Remember that the sauce will thicken as it cools.

9. Cut the loaf into inch-thick pieces, top with sauce, and serve.

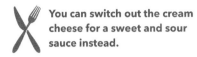
You can switch out the cream cheese for a sweet and sour sauce instead.

My love for meatballs began early. My grandparents had a community general store that happened to be just down the road from the elementary school. At lunchtime, I had the choice of going home to our own house or going to see Nan, where I had the whole entire store at my fingertips. My choice on 90 percent of those days was to go to Nan's house and have canned spaghetti and meatballs.

This love of meatballs followed me into my adult life. It's a love that I passed on to my own family. If asked, my son would almost always say that Mom's spaghetti and meatballs was his favourite, only recently to be replaced by a thick, juicy steak. My love of meatballs is alive and well in my keto world. It's the one thing I can order at an Italian restaurant fairly safely, alongside a Caesar salad. At home these days, I either have them with spaghetti squash, konjac (or shirataki) noodles, or my most favourite, a meatball bake all smothered in mozzarella cheese and marinara sauce. This recipe is one that I usually double or triple so I can freeze the extra for a quick and tasty meal.

BAKED ITALIAN MEATBALLS

SERVINGS 12   **SERVING SIZE** 3 meatballs

2	eggs
⅓	cup Parmesan, grated
2	tbsp yellow (or Dijon) mustard
1	tsp cumin
1	tsp fennel seeds, crushed
1	tsp oregano
1	tsp parsley
½	tsp basil
½	tsp rosemary
½	tsp thyme
1	medium onion, diced
3	cloves of garlic, minced
1	lb regular ground beef
½	lb ground pork
6	strips of bacon, diced

Meatless Marinara Sauce (page 232)

½	cup mozzarella, shredded
⅓	cup buffalo mozzarella, cut into 1-inch chunks

1. In a large bowl, whisk to combine eggs, cheese, mustard, and spices.

2. Add in the onion and garlic.

3. With a very light hand, mix together the beef, pork, bacon, and egg mixture. Keep in mind that the more you handle the mixture, the tougher the meatballs will be.

4. Carefully form the meat into balls. We make ours about 1.5 inches in diameter, which gives us 36 meatballs. Place in an ovenproof casserole dish.

5. Bake at 350°F for 20 minutes or until meatballs reach an internal temperature of 160°F.

6. Remove from the oven. Set oven to 375°F.

7. Pour Meatless Marinara Sauce over the meatballs, cover with shredded mozzarella, then scatter pieces of buffalo mozzarella on top.

8. Return to the oven and bake at 375°F for 10 minutes.

carbs	fibre	fat	protein
1g	.1g	30g	26.1g

Values are for the meatballs alone. Please add any toppings to your own calculations.

Beef with Broccoli is traditionally made with thick slivers of beef, but we make ours with ground beef. Served by itself or alongside a bowl of cauliflower rice, this is a great weeknight dinner for you and your family.

BEEF *with* BROCCOLI

SERVINGS 4   **SERVING SIZE** ⅔ cup

1. Add sesame oil to a deep-frying pan and heat over medium-high heat.

2. Add onion and sauté for 5 minutes or until translucent.

3. Add ground beef and cook until it begins to brown.

4. Push meat to the edges of pan and add garlic. Cook for 3-5 minutes.

5. Add remaining ingredients (except xanthan) and stir to combine.

6. Sprinkle xanthan gum into the sauce using a shaker and stir to combine.

7. Cover, reduce heat, and simmer for 5-7 minutes or until broccoli reaches desired doneness. (We like ours with just the tiniest bit of crunch.)

2   tbsp sesame oil

1   small onion, chopped

½   lb ground beef

1   cup broccoli, thickly sliced

½ to 1 cup water

½   cup beef broth

4   mushrooms, thinly sliced

3   cloves of garlic, minced

2   tbsp apple cider vinegar

2   tbsp coconut sauce

1   tsp fresh ginger, grated

1   tsp red pepper flakes

½   tsp xanthan gum

 Adjust water while cooking to maintain the level of sauce.

carbs	fibre	fat	protein
7.25g	1.25g	16g	13g

Mix up a double or triple batch of the batter and separate it into single batches before you begin coating your chicken. (Be sure to discard any leftover batter that has come into contact with chicken.) Store the extra in the freezer for even quicker breaded chicken next time.

You can boil or bake jicama wedges, then toss them in the dry batter and deep-fry them for a crispy coated wedge.

4   large boneless, skinless chicken breasts

Himalayan pink salt and pepper, to taste

2   eggs

3   tbsp water

lard for frying

FOR THE BATTER

½   cup ground pork rinds

½   cup almond flour

2   tsp garlic powder

2   tsp Himalayan pink salt

1½   tsp onion powder

1   tsp chili powder

1   tsp dried oregano

1   tsp dry mustard powder

1   tsp ground ginger

1   tsp ground thyme

½   tsp pepper

½   tsp smoked paprika

¼   tsp coriander

¼   tsp ground cumin

carbs	fibre	fat	protein
2g	1g	16g	41g

You've been craving that chicken sandwich, haven't you? The one with the battered chicken, slathered in mayonnaise, with a little bit of crunchy lettuce. I know, me too!

Ladies and gentlemen, I give you the Best-Ever Breaded Chicken burger. Our version does not have a bun, of course, but you can have it in a lettuce wrap, on Keto Bread (page 249), or do as we do and just serve it on the plate and top with Keto Mayonnaise (page 227) and shredded lettuce. We serve it with jicama fries (see the recipe for Jiggs' Dinner Poutine, page 64 or Halloumi Cheese Fries, page 63) and a delicious dollop of Creamy Keto Coleslaw (page 189). Happy eating!

BEST-EVER BREADED CHICKEN

SERVINGS 4   **SERVING SIZE** 1 yummy piece

1.   Flatten/pound the chicken breasts to an even thickness. We wrap them in plastic to avoid chicken splattering our kitchen.

2.   Lightly season the chicken with salt and pepper.

3.   Whisk together the eggs and water to made an egg wash.

4.   Let the flattened chicken sit in the egg wash while you're mixing the ingredients for the batter.

5.   Combine all ingredients for the batter.

6.   Take the chicken from the egg wash, then press into the batter mix.

7.   Shake off extra batter and drop the chicken into a 350°F deep-fryer for about 6 minutes or until the chicken reaches an internal temperature of 165°F. (Or fry in a shallow pan with melted oil just to the shoulder of the chicken, using a meat thermometer to regulate temperature.) Remember, don't leave hot oil unattended while frying.

8.   Drain cooked breaded chicken on a wire rack.

Choose boneless, skinless thighs for a juicier burger.

If you're serving with fries (we use jicama fries), cook them ahead of the chicken and set aside. Then put them in the oil for a second dip while the chicken is resting. Double frying makes them extra crispy.

Pre-keto and even pre-Bobbi and Geoff, there were two rib recipes. Friends tell us both of our versions of ribs were pretty frikkin' good. When we got together, we not only joined our lives, we also merged our rib recipes. Blazin' Baby Backs are a perfect joining of two separate recipes. We hope you enjoy.

Goes well with jicama or turnip fries.

Add a half cup of Bourbon for a real southwestern touch.

Add hot sauce if you like your ribs extra spicy.

BLAZIN' BABY BACKS

SERVINGS 4   **SERVING SIZE** half rack

1. Preheat oven to 325°F.

2. Cut each rack into thirds for easier handling.

3. Arrange ribs in a roaster bone side down, which allows the bones to serve as a natural rack. Place water, vinegar, coconut sauce, and liquid smoke into the roaster.

4. Combine spices, salt, and pepper, then sprinkle over top of the ribs.

5. Cover and bake for 2.5 hours. Check every 60 minutes to make sure there's still liquid at the bottom.

6. Remove from oven and place on a parchment-lined baking sheet. Set oven to 400°F.

7. Baste both sides of the ribs with Smokin' BBQ Sauce (page 246).

8. Return to the oven for 5 minutes.

9. Remove and drizzle with extra virgin olive oil while you turn the oven on broil. Place ribs under the broiler for no more than a couple of minutes. Keep an eye on them to make sure they only start to crisp up, not burn.

10. Serve as is or cut into pieces. These will be fall-apart goodness.

2-3 racks of baby back ribs

3-4 cups water

¼ cup cider vinegar

2 tbsp coconut sauce

1 tsp liquid smoke

2 tsp cumin

1 tsp smoked paprika

1 tsp coriander

1 tsp garlic powder

1 tsp red or Korean pepper flakes

½ tsp chipotle powder

Himalayan pink salt and pepper, to taste

Smokin' BBQ Sauce (page 246)

2 tbsp extra virgin olive oil

carbs	fibre	fat	protein
6.25g	.75g	54.5g	39g

Values do not include sauce.

A braised meat dish is a weekend favourite in the East Coast Keto kitchen. Think of a braise as being similar to a stew cooked on a simmer for hours, but with a braise there is less liquid and the cooking time is longer. Think low. Think low and slow.

Low temperature for a longer time makes your meat juicy and fall-off-the-bone tender. When you're cooking Braised Lamb Shanks, expect the house to be filled with tantalizing aromas of meat and fragrant rosemary that will have your kids and your taste buds asking, "Is it ready yet?" Braised Lamb Shanks will have you looking forward to mealtime like no other dish you've cooked.

BRAISED LAMB SHANKS

SERVINGS 4   **SERVING SIZE** 1 shank

4	lamb shanks (about 1 lb each)
	Himalayan pink salt and pepper
2	tbsp olive oil (plus 1 tbsp)
2	medium onions, chopped
2	stalks celery, chopped into 1-inch pieces
2	large carrots, peeled, cut into ¼-inch rounds
8	cloves of garlic, minced
5	tsp fresh rosemary, chopped
2	tsp fresh thyme, chopped
1½	cups dry red wine
1	cup beef broth
1	cup chicken broth
2	cups water (plus ¼ cup)
2	tsp grated lemon peel
1	tsp xanthan gum
4	sprigs fresh rosemary, for garnish

STEP 1: THE SEAR

Prepare lamb by seasoning with Himalayan pink salt and pepper on all sides of the shanks. Heat 2 tbsp oil in a large, heavy pot over medium-high heat and add shanks. Cook on all sides until brown (8-10 minutes). Remove meat from the pan and set aside.

STEP 2: THE *MIREPOIX*

Every braise has a *mirepoix*, a mixture of onion, celery, and carrot, all cooked in the drippings, and the brown/burnt bits left behind by searing the meat.

Add the extra tablespoon of oil, along with the onion, celery, carrot, garlic, and herbs to the pan and cook until near caramelized but not scorched. A quarter cup of water can be added to keep the pan from drying out.

STEP 3: DEGLAZE THE POT

Add the wine and broth to the pot and continue to cook over medium-high heat. Use a wooden spoon to scrape off any browned bits that are hanging on the side of the pot or stuck to the bottom. These are the little flavour bombs that will enrich the entire dish.

STEP 4: THE BRAISE

Preheat your oven to 300°F. Return the shanks to the pot. Add lemon peel and water to the shoulders of the meat, so that the shanks around 75 percent immersed. Cover and place in oven for 2.5 hours.

STEP 5: THE JUS

Remove the shanks from the pot and tent with aluminum foil on a plate or cutting board. Using a slotted spoon or "spider," move the onion, celery, and carrot from the pot into a bowl. Bring the remaining liquid to a boil over medium heat and slowly sprinkle some xanthan gum to thicken the sauce. Remove from heat. Sauce will thicken more as it cools. Plate the shank, spoon a few tablespoons of sauce over top, and garnish with a sprig of fresh rosemary. Enjoy!

This dish pairs well with Creamed Spinach (page 186).

 Carrots are only recommended when you're fat adapted, in moderation.

carbs	fibre	fat	protein
1.5g	0g	29g	65g

The very thought of chicken cacciatore makes me smile and brings me back to Saturday morning cartoons. I remember it being mentioned on an episode of the Flintstones. It was being billed as an upscale fancy-schmancy dish, and I just had to try it.

Since then a lot of cacciatore has graced our dining room table. This recipe only takes a few small tweaks to bring it to the keto world, but it's such a favourite of ours that it had to be included.

CHICKEN CACCIATORE

SERVINGS 6   **SERVING SIZE** 1 leg

2	tbsp bacon fat
6	chicken legs, cut into sections
½	medium onion, diced
2	cloves of garlic, minced
1	can (28 oz) San Marzano tomatoes
1	poblano pepper, roasted
1	cup bell pepper, diced
6	slices of bacon, chopped
1	cup generic tomato sauce
1	tsp smoked paprika
¼	tsp marjoram
¼	tsp oregano
¼	tsp red pepper flakes
¼	tsp thyme

Himalayan pink salt and pepper, to taste

1. Heat bacon fat over medium heat in a greased, ovenproof pan.

2. Sauté chicken until brown on all sides. Remove from the pan and set aside.

3. Add onion and garlic, and sauté until onions are translucent.

4. Add tomatoes and juice, poblano pepper, bell pepper, bacon, tomato sauce, spices, salt, and pepper.

5. Return chicken to the pan.

6. Cover and bring to a boil, then reduce heat.

7. Simmer for 20 minutes, until chicken is tender.

 Make sure your tomatoes have no added sugars.

carbs	fibre	fat	protein
15g	4g	29g	43.5g

"Crack slaw" is a warm cabbage salad, a stovetop casserole, well known in the keto community. It has a cabbage base, and you add spices to create your own flavour profile and then choose a meat (see our Crack Slaw with Chicken on page 159). The term "crack" probably comes from the sales concept of the "crack dealer approach," where you give the customer a free sample of your wares, knowing the product is just that good that they will be automatically hooked.

There are many different versions of crack slaw available online, but we think our version—which uses spinach instead of cabbage for a deeper, more earthy taste and therefore technically is not a "slaw"—tops the rest. Our own combination of seasonings and spices elevates this dish past most of the crack slaws out there. Like the saying goes, you've tried the rest, now try the best.

Try it with a splash of hot sauce and/or crème fraîche on top.

CRACK GROUND BEEF
with SPINACH

SERVINGS 2   **SERVING SIZE** 6 oz

½   lb ground beef

Himalayan pink salt and pepper, to taste

½   medium onion, chopped

2   cloves of garlic, minced

2   tbsp chili powder

1   tsp cumin

1   tsp Korean pepper flakes

1   tsp thyme

1   tsp turmeric

½   tsp coriander

14   cups apple cider vinegar

2   cups fresh spinach

1   tbsp coconut sauce

1   tbsp fish sauce

1   tbsp hot sauce

1   tsp grated ginger

5-6   mushrooms, sliced thick

12   cups water

6-8   baby tomatoes, halved

1. Brown ground beef and season with Himalayan salt and pepper to taste. Remove from pan and set aside.

2. In the same pan, sauté onion and garlic for 5 minutes or until onion is translucent.

3. Push onion and garlic to the sides of the pan and cook spices directly in the fat.

4. Stir in the vinegar, coconut sauce, fish sauce, hot sauce, and ginger.

5. Add spinach, mushrooms, and water and cover to steam until spinach has wilted, taking the time to turn the spinach so it all cooks evenly.

6. Add tomatoes and ground beef. Mix well and continue cooking for 5 minutes.

7. Serve and enjoy!

 Serve with extra hot sauce on the side for added heat.

carbs	fibre	fat	protein
18g	7.5g	13g	17.5g

This is one of Sidekick Geoff's favourite recipes. In fact, given the opportunity, I'm convinced he would eat this meal four or five nights out of seven in any given week.

A slaw is traditionally a cabbage salad, or a dish with a cabbage base. The fried cabbage in this recipe paired up with the seasoned chicken makes this an easy to whip up staple meal for any ketonian family.

CRACK SLAW *with* CHICKEN

SERVINGS 4   **SERVING SIZE** 6 oz

1. Heat oil/fat in a large sauté pan over medium heat.

2. Brown chicken and season with salt and pepper to taste. Remove from pan and set aside.

3. Add cabbage, green onion, garlic, and water to the pan and cover. Cook until cabbage reaches desired tenderness.

4. Stir in the vinegar, coconut sauce, hot sauce, Swerve, and ginger.

5. Add chicken, mix well, and serve!

2   tbsp extra virgin olive oil or bacon fat

1   lb boneless chicken thigh or breast, patted dry and chopped into thin strips

Himalayan salt and pepper, to taste

2   cups grated cabbage

½   cup water

¼   cup white vinegar

3   green onions, sliced

2   cloves of garlic, minced

2   tbsp coconut sauce

1   tsp hot sauce

1   tsp Swerve

½   tsp minced ginger

Serve with hot sauce on the side for added heat.

carbs	fibre	fat	protein
7.8g	2.9g	23.9g	23.1g

FOR THE CHICKEN

2-3   tbsp avocado oil

14-16 chicken thighs

3   cloves of garlic, minced

2   tbsp butter

Himalayan salt and pepper,
to taste

1   tbsp garam masala

4   cup chicken stock

FOR THE SAUCE

1   can (28 oz) San Marzano
       tomatoes, diced

¼   cup butter, melted

1   large white onion, diced

3   cloves of garlic, minced

2   tbsp chili powder

2   tbsp finely grated fresh
       ginger

2   tbsp lemon juice

1   tbsp coconut sauce

1   tbsp fish sauce

1   tbsp garam masala

1   tbsp red pepper flakes

1   tsp ground cardamom

1   tsp ground coriander

1   tsp ground cumin

1   tsp freshly ground nutmeg

1   tsp ground turmeric

Sweetener, to taste

1   cup whipping cream (35%)

½   cup coconut milk

Our version of spicy and pungent butter chicken is one of our favourite recipes to cook up together on a lazy weekend day spent in the kitchen. We cook breakfast and after clean up, we merge right into cooking again.

Chicken breast can be used, but the thighs will add more flavour to the dish and will also help provide more healthy fats to your macros.

We usually cook this one into a double or even triple batch and freeze the extra sauce or combined chicken and sauce for a quick and tasty meal down the road.

EASY BUTTER CHICKEN

SERVINGS 8   **SERVING SIZE** 2 thighs

1. Heat avocado oil in a large roasting pan over medium-high heat.

2. Add the chicken thighs and sauté until brown, then flip and brown other side.

3. Remove the pan from heat and add garlic, butter, salt and pepper, garam masala, and stock to the roasting pan. Cover.

4. Bake at 275°F for 1 hour.

5. When chicken is cooked, remove thighs from the pan and cut them into 1-inch chunks. Set aside.

6. Add sauce ingredients to the stock in the pan, with the exception of the last three: sweetener, cream, and coconut milk.

7. Stir to combine and simmer over medium heat for 15 minutes until the sauce begins to thicken.

8. Let sauce cool then partially blend with an immersion blender, being careful to leave small pieces of tomato and onion for texture.

9. Stir in chicken, sweetener, cream, and milk, then simmer for 5 minutes to blend the flavours and finish the dish.

carbs	fibre	fat	protein
8.4g	1.25g	28.6g	6.375g

Fettuccine Alfredo with Sautéed Chicken Breast and Bacon is a deeply satisfying, crowd-pleasing dinner that is quick and easy to make. The creamy homemade Alfredo sauce, amplified by the bacon, is the feature in this family favourite meal. Make sure you add the nutmeg. It sounds out of place, but it's really that hidden little ingredient that makes the dish go OMG! Delish.

FETTUCCINE ALFREDO *with* SAUTÉED CHICKEN BREAST AND BACON

SERVINGS 4   **SERVING SIZE** 6 oz

- 2 tbsp butter
- 2 boneless, skinless chicken breasts, cut into thin strips
- 1 clove of garlic, minced
- 1 green onion, chopped
- 3 strips of bacon, precooked and chopped into pieces
- ½ tsp parsley
- ¼ tsp thyme

Himalayan salt and pepper, to taste

konjac noodles, well rinsed, drained, and cut in half (we use NuPasta)

FOR THE SAUCE

- 1 tbsp butter
- 7 cloves of garlic, minced or grated
- 1½ cup whipping cream (35%)
- ¾ cup Parmesan, grated
- ¼ tsp thyme

Himalayan salt and pepper, to taste

nutmeg (dash)

FOR GARNISH

- 1 piece of bacon, precooked and chopped

FOR THE CHICKEN

1. Heat butter in a large sauté pan.
2. Sauté the chicken for 5 minutes.
3. Add garlic and cook over low heat.
4. Add green onion, bacon, parsley, thyme, salt, and pepper, and stir to combine.
5. Cook until the chicken starts to slightly brown.
6. Set aside.

FOR THE ALFREDO SAUCE

1. Melt butter in a medium saucepan over medium heat. Add minced garlic and sauté for about 1 minute.
2. Add cream. Bring to a gentle simmer, then continue to simmer for about 10 minutes, or until sauce starts to thicken. Be careful, this can easily bubble over.
3. Reduce heat to low. Slowly whisk in Parmesan and thyme. Whisk until smooth.
4. Add Himalayan salt, pepper, and nutmeg, and simmer for 5 minutes.

carbs	fibre	fat	protein
2g	2g	55g	30g

 If sauce is thicker than you like, add a little extra cream.

PUTTING IT ALL TOGETHER

1. Add the konjac noodles to a dry pan and dry fry (i.e., no oil or water) for 5 minutes.

2. Add the chicken to the pan and cook for 5 minutes.

3. Slowly spoon on the Alfredo sauce, being careful not to drown the noodles. (As there are only two of us, and the recipe yields enough for four people, we hold back some sauce and freeze it for another meal.)

4. Simmer the noodles and sauce for 5 minutes, then plate.

5. Garnish with bacon and serve.

2   tbsp bacon fat or oil

1   medium onion, chopped

1   lb regular ground beef

½   lb ground pork

6   strips of bacon, chopped

2   cups orange and/or red peppers, chopped

4   cloves of garlic, minced

2   tbsp coconut sauce
     (as soy sauce substitute)

4   tbsp chili powder

2   tbsp cumin

1   tbsp garlic

1   tbsp onion powder

1   tbsp red pepper flakes

½   tbsp coriander

2   tsp Himalayan pink salt

1   tsp freshly ground black pepper

1   tsp smoked paprika

1   tsp thyme

3   tbsp Lakanto brown sugar substitute

1   cup chicken stock, to deglaze

1   can (340 g) corned beef (a.k.a. bully beef)

375 ml canned black olives, chopped

3-4 dashes of Tabasco or hot sauce

1   can (28 oz) San Marzano tomatoes

TOPPINGS

grated cheddar

sour cream

green onions, chopped

hot sauce

One of the biggest worries for ketonians is what to serve a crowd. How do we protect our keto way of eating while satisfying the appetites of many? On Super Bowl day, this keto-licious meal will keep you within your macros and also satisfy those meat-etarians that will be gathering on your couch.

It took us a while to try keto chili. We were afraid that it just wouldn't hold up to its predecessor, our brown sugar chili. Not to mention that beans were not a part of our life anymore. Who eats chili without beans? Apparently, we do! After a brainstorming session, we identified a couple of ingredients that would take our ordinary chili and lift it to the flavour height we were used to. We were delighted with the end result.

GAME DAY CHILI

SERVINGS 9   **SERVING SIZE** 1 bowl

1. Heat oil in a large pot over medium heat.

2. Sauté onions until translucent.

3. Add ground beef and pork, breaking meat apart as it cooks.

4. When the meat is mostly cooked (but not yet browned) push it to the edges of the pan and add bacon and peppers to the centre of the pan. Cook until the bacon is mostly cooked and the peppers are soft, then combine the peppers with the meat.

5. Push the meat mixture back to the sides of the pot and add garlic and coconut sauce to the centre. Cook for 3 minutes, then combine the garlic with the main mixture.

6. Reduce heat to a simmer. Push meat mixture back to the sides of the pan one more time and stir spices and seasonings one by one into the oil. Once the spices have bloomed (i.e., after about 30 seconds), integrate them into the meat mix.

7. Add sweetener.

carbs	fibre	fat	protein
8.6g	6.6g	31g	23.3g

Values do not include any toppings. Please calculate your own macros for any toppings added to your bowl.

8. Deglaze pan with chicken stock.

9. Mix in corned (i.e., "bully") beef, olives, and Tabasco sauce.

10. Add tomatoes (including juice) and taste. Adjust spices, salt, and pepper to taste. (We like ours extra spicy so we usually add more.)

11. Simmer for 20 minutes, scoop into bowls, and add desired toppings. Serve with Savoury Cheesy Biscuits (page 200).

Many people who have spent time down south have tasted Jamaican meat pies and fallen in love with the brazen flavour profile created by curries and hot peppers. It's a meal or treat that is loved the world over.

Sidekick Geoff and I had the pleasure of being married in Jamaica, so these hot and pungent tastes hold a special place in our hearts, as well as in our tummies. Adjust the spices to suit your own tastes in this one.

These can be made into patties, but as the dough doesn't have the same glutenous stretch as regular non-keto pastry, we prefer to save ourselves the aggravation of trying to work the dough into turnover shapes and just make our version into a pot pie.

JAMAICAN PATTIE POT PIE

SERVINGS 4   **SERVING SIZE** ¼ of the pie

1. Add bacon fat and ground meat to a large sauté pan on medium heat and begin to brown.
2. After 5 minutes, push meat to the sides of the pan and add chopped onion to the oil in the centre.
3. After 5 minutes, push the onion to the sides with the meat and add garlic and peppers to the oil in the centre.
4. After 5 minutes, push the peppers to the sides and add Swerve, spices, salt, and pepper to the centre of the pan.
5. After 5 minutes, combine all ingredients and reduce heat.
6. Add water and cover. Simmer for 10 minutes.
7. Let cool.

PUTTING IT ALL TOGETHER

The final steps in putting this dish together depend on your preference. We lined the bottom of a casserole dish with a single layer of pastry and prebaked the shell according to the pastry instructions. We then let all ingredients cool and placed the meat filling in the shell and topped it with a crust, baking one last time according to the pastry instructions.

You can do a version with just a top, where you omit the lower prebaked shell, and you can also separate the dough into smaller sections and roll them into individual pies or turnovers.

 Use a fork for a quick and easy, fuss-free pastry edge.

FOR THE FILLING

1	lb ground pork (or beef, or a combination of both)
2	tbsp bacon fat or extra virgin olive oil
½	medium onion, chopped
2	cloves of garlic, chopped
3	jalapeno peppers, chopped

red pepper (habanero or Scotch bonnet), chopped, to taste

¼	cup confectioner's Swerve
2	tsp ground coriander
2	tsp ground cumin
1	tsp ancho chili powder
1	tsp curry powder
1	tsp dried thyme
1	tsp garlic powder
1	tsp red pepper flakes
½	tsp allspice
½	tsp turmeric

Himalayan pink salt and pepper, to taste

½	cup water

FOR THE CRUST

Use ECK Pie Crust recipe (page 218) but omit the Swerve and add 1 tsp turmeric.

I roll the crust up on the very edge, creating a lip that is double or triple thickness of the rest of the crust. Then I use my finger and thumb to gently pinch a decorative edge on the outside of the pie. While you're working the kinks out of your pastry is a great time to experiment with the crust edge.

carbs	fibre	fat	protein
9.5g	40.5g	36.25g	20g

FOR THE NOODLES

Use the Pizza Crust recipe on page 240.

FOR THE FILLING

2 tbsp extra virgin olive oil or bacon fat

1 lb regular ground beef

1 medium onion, minced

3 cloves of garlic, minced

1½ tsp oregano

1 tsp basil

½ tsp parsley

½ tsp red pepper flakes

½ tsp rosemary

½ tsp thyme

1½ cups San Marzano tomatoes (we blend our tomatoes so the resulting sauce is smooth)

2 tbsp Lakanto brown sugar substitute or equivalent keto sweetener to taste

6 tbsp ricotta cheese (full fat)

½ cup mozzarella, shredded

⅓ cup buffalo mozzarella (optional)

carbs 95g	fibre 1g	fat 36g	protein 36g

This low-carb, keto, and luxurious lasagna was a while in the making. Our original recipe had traditional pasta, which at the time we thoroughly enjoyed. Then we gradually switched those carby pasta noodles to sheets of thinly sliced tofu in our first attempt to get healthy. (We later discovered soy/tofu is inflammatory and not keto recommended.) The recipe made the final switch when we started our keto way of eating. The idea for our keto pasta came from our own version of pizza dough. What if we made the same dough, but enclosed it between two sheets of parchment paper and rolled it out thinner with a rolling pin? Wouldn't that same thick pizza base become a thin layer of lasagna noodles?

With the help of this new discovery, our keto kitchen is now complete with the cozy comfort of a hot and cheesy plate of lasagna.

Serve this keto lasagna with a Caesar salad (see our Caesar Dressing on page 211) and you've got a super tasty meal that fills up your belly in a warm and delicious way, and after you're finished, you don't have to feel the least bit guilty.

LASAGNA   **SERVINGS** 6   **SERVING SIZE** 1 piece

FOR THE NOODLES

1. Preheat oven to 350°F.

2. Prepare two large sheets of parchment paper (the size of your biggest baking sheet).

3. Spread the dough mixture onto the first sheet of parchment paper, forming a nice even layer and leaving room around the edges of the parchment for the noodle dough to spread.

4. Top with second parchment, forming a sandwich with the dough in the middle.

5. Slowly roll out the dough between the two sheets.

6. Place your dough sandwich on the baking sheet and bake on the middle rack for 10 minutes.

7. Flip your dough sandwich and bake for 10 more minutes.

8. Cool your "pasta" for 10 minutes and then cut into sections to fit your pan. Set aside.

FOR THE FILLING

1. Heat extra virgin olive oil or fat in a large frying pan over medium heat.

2. Add ground beef and onion. Cook until onion is translucent.

3. Push meat mixture to the sides and add garlic directly to the centre of the pan. Cook for 2 minutes, then mix with the other ingredients.

4. Push meat mixture to the side again and place your spices directly into the oil in the bottom of the pan for 1 minute. Combine with meat mixture and cook over medium-high heat until meat starts to brown.

5. Add tomatoes and simmer for 2 minutes.

6. Add sweetener to the sauce and simmer for 10 more minutes.

PUTTING IT ALL TOGETHER

1. Pour meat sauce into the bottom of a 9 x 9 baking pan. Top with a layer of noodles.

2. Top with ricotta cheese and then a third of the ground beef mixture and then a second layer of noodles.

3. Add the remaining ground beef mixture.

4. Cover with another noodle layer and mozzarella cheese.

5. Cut the buffalo mozzarella into chunks and place on top.

6. Bake for 20 minutes. Allow to cool for 20 minutes before serving.

If you don't have a rolling pin, you can use a glass or a can to flatten the dough.

The noodle dough can be made the night before and refrigerated.

sidekick recipe

This dish pairs well with Creamed Spinach (page 186).

3 tbsp olive oil

4 English cut short beef ribs (about 1 lb per person)

Himalayan pink salt and pepper, to taste

2 medium onions, chopped

1 cup celery, chopped

2 large carrots, peeled, cut into ¼-inch rounds

8 cloves of garlic, minced

2 tsp fresh thyme, chopped

¼ cup water (optional)

½ bottle dry red wine (i.e., 375 ml)

1 cup chicken broth

1 cup beef broth

2 cups water

1 tsp xanthan gum

fresh parsley, for garnish

carbs	fibre	fat	protein
1.25g	.25g	68g	53g

We fell in love with Low and Slow Beef Short Ribs at a foodie festival. It was a small plates event, but they were so delicious that I'm sure I could have eaten a whole potful all by myself.

At home, we quickly dug in and figured out how to master this dish on our own. We fell in love all over again with the tender braised beef, the mirepoix veggies, and the delicate sauce.

Fast forward to our keto lifestyle; we knew this had to be one of the recipes that we would ketofy. Low and Slow Beef Short Ribs will not disappoint. They will knock it out of the park at any family feast and also wow your guests at a potluck dinner.

The key to this dish is the selection and cut of the ribs. You'll have to go to the meat counter and ask to have short ribs cut for you. The ones you'll find on the shelf will be flanken cut, which are cut across the bone, giving you a little slice of all the bones. You want English cut, where there is one bone per piece, about two inches long. They tend to hold their shape even after a long braise and make an impressive presentation. Ask for pieces around two by four inches.

LOW AND SLOW BEEF SHORT RIBS

SERVINGS 4   **SERVING SIZE** 1 rack

STEP 1: THE SEAR

1. Preheat oven to 300°F.

2. Heat 2 tablespoons of the oil in a large ovenproof dish on the stovetop.

3. Brown the ribs. Get a good sear on the meat to lock in the juices.

4. Sprinkle Himalayan pink salt and pepper on all sides of the ribs.

5. Set aside.

STEP 2: THE *MIREPOIX*

Add the remaining oil (1 tbsp), along with the onion, celery, carrot, garlic, and thyme to the pan and cook until onion is translucent but not scorched. To help with the cooking process, a quarter cup of water can be added.

STEP 3: DEGLAZE THE POT

Add the wine and broth to the pot and continue to cook over medium-high heat. Use a wooden spoon to scrape off any browned bits that are hanging on the side of the pot or stuck to the bottom.

STEP 4: THE BRAISE

Return the ribs to the pot, along with any juices that are left in the bowl or tray. Add water until the liquid is up to "the shoulders" of the meat (i.e., three-quarters of the way up). Cover and place in oven for 2.5 hours.

STEP 5: THE JUS

Remove the ribs from the pan and cover with foil or plastic wrap. Using a slotted spoon, remove the vegetables and set aside. Bring the remaining liquid to a boil over medium heat and slowly sprinkle xanthan gum to thicken the sauce. Remove from heat; it will thicken more as it cools. Plate the ribs, spoon a few tablespoons of sauce over the top, and garnish with a sprig of fresh parsley. Enjoy!

If you grew up in Newfoundland, you're likely familiar with canned meatballs and gravy. It was a staple in most households, especially one with teenagers. It was a quick and easy meal. Just warm it up, throw it on top of a plate of shoestring fries, and all the kids were happy.

Our Mooseballs and Gravy is a low-carb and healthier version of those meatballs. Our meatballs call for moose, but you can use regular ground beef or a combination of beef and pork. Combine this with some daikon or jicama fries and you're all set.

MOOSEBALLS AND GRAVY

SERVINGS 4   **SERVING SIZE** 5 meatballs

FOR THE MEATBALLS

1	lb ground moose
½	cup whipping cream (35%)
⅓	cup pork rind, crushed
1	large egg
1	medium onion, finely chopped
3	large cloves of garlic, minced
2	tbsp fresh parsley, finely chopped
1	tbsp butter
2	tsp olive oil
1	tsp Himalayan pink salt
¼	tsp pepper

FOR THE GRAVY

1	cup beef broth
1	cup vegetable broth
¼	cup cream cheese
2	tbsp coconut sauce
1	tsp Dijon mustard
½	tsp thyme

Himalayan pink salt and pepper, to taste

FOR THE MEATBALLS

1. Combine all ingredients with a very light hand. (The more you handle the mixture, the tougher the meatballs will be.)

2. Carefully form the meat into 20 balls about an inch and a half in diameter.

3. Sauté meatballs in a large frying pan over medium heat until cooked through, turning them often to make sure they cook on all sides.

FOR THE GRAVY

1. Deglaze meatball pan with broth, then simmer.

2. Add cream cheese, coconut sauce, and mustard. Whisk until smooth.

3. Slowly add xanthan gum, keeping in mind that it will thicken more as it cools.

4. Add thyme, and salt and pepper to taste.

carbs	fibre	fat	protein
8.75g	1g	60g	38g

Paprika Pork Chops is a super simple recipe with super delicious flavour. It's a quick family supper or for when company is coming.

Paprika is one of those spices that everybody has in their cupboard, but in reality, most use it very little, just to sprinkle on devilled eggs or a casserole. Paprika Pork Chops do a great job of showcasing the smoky sweet heat of the peppers from which it originated. Our preference is smoked paprika for that smoky taste.

PAPRIKA PORK CHOPS

SERVINGS 4   **SERVING SIZE** 1 chop

4	bone-in pork chops
2	tbsp bacon fat or extra virgin olive oil
1¼	cup chicken broth
¼	cup apple cider vinegar
2	tbsp coconut sauce
2	cloves of garlic, minced
2	tsp smoked paprika
½	tsp ginger, grated
½	tsp oregano
½	tsp thyme

Himalayan pink salt and pepper, to taste

1. Dry pork chops on a paper towel.

2. Place pork and bacon fat in an ovenproof roasting pan on medium heat on the stovetop and brown pork on both sides.

3. Mix liquid ingredients together and add to the sauté pan. Liquid should come to the shoulders of the pork chops and not completely cover them.

4. Add the garlic and ginger to the liquid.

5. Mix all dry ingredients, sprinkle over pork chops, then cover the pan and transfer it to the oven.

6. Bake at 350°F for 15 minutes, then remove the cover and bake for an additional 5 minutes or until pork reaches internal temperature of 145°F.

carbs	fibre	fat	protein
3.5g	.25g	24g	38.5g

Hubby Geoff has been a sucker for BBQ steak his whole life. He thought the only way to cook a steak was to slather it with BBQ sauce and throw it on the barbie. That's until he tasted this Rib-eye Steak with French Garlic Cheese Sauce.

Company is coming and you want a flawless, stress-free steak recipe? Our Rib-eye Steak with French Garlic Cheese Sauce fits the bill. This recipe can be prepared ahead of time and held in the oven till you're ready to eat. It will impress your guests, and you won't have to spend the night outside alone at the BBQ.

RIB-EYE STEAK *with* FRENCH GARLIC CHEESE SAUCE

SERVINGS 2   **SERVING SIZE** 1 steak

1   cup red wine

½   cup soft French garlic cheese (We use Boursin.)

2   rib-eye steaks

Himalayan salt and pepper, to taste

3   tbsp butter

1. In a saucepan, heat the wine over medium-high heat until it starts to reduce.

2. Add cheese to the wine reduction. Simmer the sauce until reduced by about half. Set aside.

3. Season steak on both sides with salt and pepper.

4. Melt butter in a pan and sauté steak over medium heat to the desired doneness, flipping once to brown on both sides. Set aside to rest, uncovered.

5. Add cheese and wine reduction into the steak drippings and reduce heat to simmer. Whisk to incorporate.

6. Slice steak into diagonal strips against the grain of the meat.

7. Plate the steak and cover with sauce, or serve sauce on the side.

Cook a ¾-inch thick steak for approx. 2-3 minutes each side for rare, approx. 4 minutes each side for medium, and approx. 5-6 minutes each side for well done.

Sauce will thicken as it cools.

carbs	fibre	fat	protein
3.5g	0g	72.5g	39g

Salsa Chicken is our go-to recipe when we want an easy meal that's both satisfying and quick to make. We usually use boneless, skinless chicken breast, but you can use any cut of chicken or even pork for this recipe. Using chicken thighs will up your fat intake and bring bigger flavour.

The rich southwestern flavours in this salsa chicken can also be obtained by opening a jar of store-bought salsa, but we prefer the deep flavours of our homemade Saucy Salsa (page 244) to top off this dish. Add a spoonful of sour cream and you're in Mexican culinary heaven, right in your own home.

SALSA CHICKEN

SERVINGS 2   **SERVING SIZE** 1 chicken breast

1. Preheat oven to 350°F.

2. Pat chicken dry with a paper towel.

3. Combine spices, spread mix on a piece of foil or parchment, and roll chicken to coat evenly.

4. Place chicken on a parchment-lined baking sheet.

5. Cover each piece of chicken with a couple tablespoons of salsa and bake for 35 minutes.

6. Remove from oven and cover with cheese.

7. Return to oven and cook for additional 10 minutes or until cheese is melted.

8. Top with your favourite toppings.

2   boneless, skinless chicken breasts

chicken spice mix (recipe below)

4   tbsp Saucy Salsa (page 244)

½   cup cheddar, grated

FOR THE CHICKEN SPICE MIX

2   tsp chili powder

1   tsp coriander

1   tsp cumin

1   tsp garlic powder

1   tsp Himalayan pink salt

1   tsp onion powder

1   tsp smoked paprika

TOPPINGS

sour cream or crème fraîche

salsa

hot sauce

guacamole (page 219)

 Chicken thighs will up your fat intake and bring bigger flavour.

Values do not include sauce or toppings. See Saucy Salsa recipe (page 244), and please calculate your macros based on any toppings you use.

carbs	fibre	fat	protein
5g	2g	37g	31.5g

SIDES

Our Broccoli Salad is one of those recipes that will work with any meal. It's perfect alongside an old-fashioned cold plate, will steal the show at a backyard BBQ, and is also the perfect companion to a roast (chicken, pork, or beef). Make sure you use the stems of the broccoli as well. We peel the outer rind of the stems and then cut them into a medium dice. They add an extra texture and crunch to the dish.

The traditional broccoli salad has raisins and pine nuts, but we leave them out of the keto version and they're not even missed. This yummy, family-friendly side dish is a guilt-free indulgence.

BROCCOLI SALAD SERVINGS 4

1 head broccoli, chopped into florets or bite-sized pieces

6 slices crispy bacon, chopped

½ cup cheddar, cubed

¼ cup onion, chopped (optional)

¾ cup Keto Mayonnaise (page 227)

2 tbsp apple cider vinegar

Stevia or equivalent, to taste

Himalayan salt and pepper, to taste

½ tsp red pepper flakes, or to taste

1. Combine broccoli florets, bacon, cheddar, and onion in a large bowl.

2. In a separate bowl, whisk together mayo, vinegar, sweetener, salt, pepper, and red pepper flakes until smooth and well combined.

3. Pour dressing over broccoli and toss to combine.

4. Use right away or cover and refrigerate for up to a week.

carbs	fibre	fat	protein
2.5g	1g	61g	5.5g

If you ever enjoyed uber silky and creamy mashed potatoes in a high-end restaurant in pre-keto days, there is a chance that it wasn't even potatoes but celeriac purée instead.

Celeriac, or celery root, is a variety of celery that has been cultivated for its edible root. It's a low-carb root vegetable that can replace potatoes in many dishes.

We simmer our celeriac in a combination of water and 35% cream to help to bring out the mellow flavours of the root. The added garlic and cream cheese tag-team to up the elegance level of this dish. One taste of this purée and you will wonder why you didn't try this veggie sooner.

CELERIAC ROOT PURÉE

SERVINGS 4   **SERVING SIZE** ½ cup

1. Bring water, cream, and salt to a boil in a large saucepan over medium-high heat.

2. Add celery root cubes and garlic and bring to boil. Reduce heat to low-medium and simmer for 20 minutes or until cubes are tender.

3. Drain and move cubes to a Magic Bullet or blender.

4. Add butter and cream cheese and puree until smooth.

5. Adjust salt and pepper to taste.

6. Sprinkle with chopped fresh herbs and serve.

1½	cups water
½	cup whipping cream (35%)
1	tsp salt
1	large celeriac/celery root, approx. 2 cups peeled, cut into 1-inch cubes
4	cloves of garlic, quartered
1	tbsp butter
1	oz cream cheese
¼	tsp fresh ground pepper
1	tbsp chopped fresh chives, thyme, or parsley

 When you peel the celeriac, carefully dig out any cracks and crevices that could have soil or dirt.

carbs	fibre	fat	protein
6g	.5g	64g	16g

Creamed spinach, for me, brings to mind Popeye with his can of muscle-bulging spinach. Even though Popeye was a big fan, we don't think there is a lot of flavour in most canned versions of creamed spinach. Ours is delicately spiced to bring out the maximum flavour of the spinach and to provide you with a side dish that your people will love.

CREAMED SPINACH

SERVINGS 4   **SERVING SIZE** 4 oz

3   tbsp butter

1   medium onion, minced

2   cloves of garlic, minced

1   tsp cumin

1   tsp red pepper flakes

⅛   tsp garam masala

Himalayan pink salt and pepper, to taste

1   cup whipping cream (35%)

2   oz cream cheese

12   oz fresh spinach, or one package frozen

½   cup water

½   cup Gruyère or Parmesan, grated

3   slices of bacon, crumbled

1. Heat butter in a sauté pan over medium-high heat.

2. Sauté onion for 5 minutes or until translucent.

3. Add garlic and continue to cook for 5 minutes.

4. Push onion and garlic to the sides of the pan and cook spices and seasonings directly in the oil in the middle of the pan.

5. Lower heat to low and simmer for 5 minutes.

6. Add cream, cream cheese, spinach, and water and cover. Simmer until spinach is wilted and water is cooked off.

7. Remove from the pan and top with shredded cheese and bacon.

carbs	fibre	fat	protein
6.5g	2.25g	42g	10g

Growing up, we were served grated carrot and cabbage with dressing from a bottle. Nowadays, we'd rather make our own coleslaw so we know what we're eating. We highly recommend our Creamy Keto Coleslaw with our Best-Ever Breaded Chicken and our Deep-Fried Fish (and Chips).

Sometimes a meal just isn't complete without a serving of coleslaw on the side, or even on top! Next time you make a burger, dollop a generous spoonful of our Creamy Keto Coleslaw over the top and you'll be pleasantly surprised. After trying it, you won't want your burgers any other way!

CREAMY KETO COLESLAW

SERVINGS 8   **SERVING SIZE** ½ cup

¼	head cabbage
⅓	cup Keto Mayonnaise (page 227)
1	tbsp avocado or olive oil
1	tsp Dijon mustard
1	tsp lemon juice
1	tsp Swerve or equivalent sweetener, or to taste
½	tsp garlic powder
½	tsp onion powder
¼	tsp celery seed
¼	tsp coriander
¼	tsp cumin
¼	tsp smoked paprika

Himalayan salt and pepper, to taste

1. Chop the cabbage into thin slices, or grate using a coarse grater.

2. Mix remaining ingredients together in a bowl.

3. Pour dressing over the prepared cabbage. Toss to combine.

4. Chill and serve.

carbs	fibre	fat	protein
2.75g	1g	17g	.5g

We know Brussels sprouts are not a favourite of many, but maybe that's because you haven't found the best way to prepare them yet!

Our Deep-Fried Brussels Sprouts will give you crispy crunch, a tangy sweet, and the tiniest taste of spicy, all in one bite. Make sure you don't discard the single leaves, they make the most delightful little crispy treats. You can serve them to your favorite guest, but we suggest you gobble them up yourself as chef's treat before you serve the others.

DEEP-FRIED BRUSSELS SPROUTS

SERVINGS 4   **SERVING SIZE** 4 oz

1-1½ lbs Brussels sprouts

1 tbsp Swerve or equivalent sweetener

1 tsp Korean or red pepper flakes

Himalayan salt and pepper, to taste

1. Half or quarter the sprouts, depending on their size.

2. Deep-fry (or shallow fry) the sprouts at 350°F until they are golden brown with the single leaves crispy but not burned, about 3-4 minutes per batch.

3. With a slotted spoon, transfer the fried sprouts to a bowl.

4. Add Swerve, red pepper flakes, and salt and pepper.

5. Toss to combine. Serve right away.

carbs	fibre	fat	protein
16g	7g	11g	6g

 These are best served right out of the deep-fryer. If you need to hold them over, keep warm in a 175-200°F oven.

Caesar salad has become a bit of a boring same old, same old side dish, especially within the ketogenic community. But have you ever had Grilled Bok Choy Caesar Salad?

The warm and slightly charred greens add a depth of flavour and take the Caesar salad to a whole new height. Switch out the bok choy for romaine if you'd like to take this warm Caesar back a little closer to traditional. Your guests will enjoy it either way.

GRILLED BOK CHOY CAESAR SALAD

SERVINGS 2   **SERVING SIZE** 1 head

FOR THE BOK CHOY

1. Preheat grill to 350°F or medium setting.
1. Slice bok choy in half lengthwise.
3. Brush the sliced bok choy with olive oil and season with pepper flakes, Himalayan pink salt, and pepper.
4. Place the bok choy on the grill, cut side down.
5. Cook until the leaves are starting to slightly crisp at the edges.
6. Flip the bok choy and cook for 2 more minutes, taking care not to burn the leaves. They should be slightly charred with grill marks, but not burned.

PUTTING IT ALL TOGETHER

1. Plate the bok choy.
2. Drizzle each section with Caesar Dressing. We zigzag the sauce over the top to create an artistic presentation.
3. Finish each plate with pieces of bacon, pork rinds, and Parmesan, arranging them on top.
4. Serve while warm.

FOR THE BOK CHOY

2   heads of baby bok choy (or 1 regular size)

extra virgin olive oil

1   tsp Korean pepper flakes

Himalayan pink salt and pepper, to taste

Caesar Dressing (page 211)

FOR GARNISH

bacon, fried crispy and cut into ½-inch squares

pork rinds, crumbled into crouton-sized pieces

Parmesan, grated or curled into ribbons

carbs	fibre	fat	protein
4.1g	2g	58g	13g

These are southern-style hash browns, diced instead of shredded and formed into a patty. The celeriac root is a perfect fit for these delectable little crunchy nuggets. We pre-boil it so the inside is already perfectly cooked and we just have to fry it up to get the outsides good and crispy. We love this on the side of any meat dish, whether it's for breakfast, lunch, or supper. Serve warm with Kwick Keto Ketchup (page 228) on the side.

KETO HASH BROWNS

SERVINGS 4

1½ cups water

½ cup whipping cream (35%)

1 tsp salt

1 large celeriac/celery root (approx. 1 pound), peeled, cut into 1-inch cubes

4 cloves of garlic, quartered

1 tbsp butter or oil for frying

½ tsp chili powder

½ tsp garlic powder

¼ tsp fresh ground pepper

1. Bring water, cream, and salt to a boil in a large saucepan over medium-high heat.

2. Add celery root cubes and garlic and bring to boil. Reduce heat to low-medium and simmer for 20 minutes, or until cubes are tender.

3. Drain and let cool.

4. Add oil to a medium sauté pan over medium heat.

5. Quarter the celery root cubes and place them in the pan.

6. Keep the celery root moving in the pan to ensure all sides brown. The cubes are already cooked so we're just crisping up the outside for crunch.

7. Cook until the hash browns reach your desired hue of golden brown. Add chili powder and garlic powder before turning off the heat, and give the hash browns one last toss/stir to incorporate these spices.

8. Adjust salt and pepper to taste and enjoy!

carbs	fibre	fat	protein
6.5g	5g	64g	16g

When you peel the celeriac, carefully dig out any cracks and crevices that could have soil or dirt.

This Parmesan Garlic Spaghetti Squash was a surprise to us. In hindsight, I'm not sure why—we love all the components separately, but there was something telling me that we wouldn't like them combined together as a dish. Even as we were putting the ingredients together, I still had doubts. It didn't look like much even as we pulled it from the oven. Typical cheesy casserole baked in a spaghetti squash shell.

The proof was in the tasting with this one. While we had always enjoyed spaghetti squash before this, it was Parmesan Garlic Spaghetti Squash that made it dance like no one was watching. We finally found a recipe that took the lowly spaghetti squash and made it frikkin' amazing. We hope you enjoy it too!

PARMESAN GARLIC SPAGHETTI SQUASH

SERVINGS 2   **SERVING SIZE** half a squash

1   spaghetti squash

1   tbsp olive oil, plus oil for the brush

Himalayan pink salt and pepper, to taste

2-3 cloves of garlic, minced

1   cup chicken stock

1   tbsp fresh parsley, finely chopped

1   tsp smoked paprika

Himalayan pink salt and freshly ground pepper

½   cup Parmesan, grated

⅓   cup crème fraîche or sour cream

parsley, for garnish

1   tbsp butter

1. Preheat oven to 375°F.

2. Cut the squash lengthwise and scoop out all the seeds and loose strands.

3. Brush on a coating of olive oil and then season to taste with Himalayan pink salt and pepper.

4. Place the spaghetti squash on a baking sheet cut side up and roast for about 45 minutes or until all the strands are soft.

5. Meanwhile, heat 1 tbsp olive oil in a sauté pan.

6. Add garlic and cook for 2 minutes.

7. Add stock, parsley, paprika, salt, and pepper and bring to a boil.

8. Add Parmesan and crème fraîche, reserving a little Parm to top off the dish. Immediately turn off the heat and continue to stir. Set aside.

carbs 9.5g	fibre 2g	fat 0g	protein 13g

9. When the squash is cooked, use a fork to scrape out the strands of cooked squash, reserving the shells.

10. Add the squash to the sauce and combine thoroughly.

11. Transfer the combined ingredients back to the squash shells and top with reserved cheese and a sprinkle of parsley.

12. Return the dressed squash to the oven and roast until the cheese melts.

13. Remove from the oven and let sit for about 10 minutes so it slightly cools.

14. Top each serving with a pat of butter for extra healthy fats and flavour.

Sometimes it's the simplest ingredients that create the most delightful taste. Sautéed Cabbage with Bacon just happens to be one of those dishes.

Two of the favourite ingredients of many ketonians come together as a marriage made in heaven. Sautéed Cabbage with Bacon can be used as a side dish, but our preference is to add a source of meat (e.g., sliced chicken breast) to this dish and use it as a stand-alone meal. Switch up the flavour profile to make it a whole new dish every time. (See our Flavour Profiles, Appendix A.)

SAUTÉED CABBAGE *with* BACON

SERVINGS 2

1. Sauté the bacon in a large pan until it reaches your level of desired crispness. Remove from the pan and set aside. Reserve bacon fat.

2. Add the onion to the bacon fat and cook until translucent, about 3-5 minutes.

3. Add the garlic and continue to cook for 1 minute.

4. Stir in the cabbage and vinegar and continue to cook for about 10 minutes. Add spices, salt, and pepper.

5. Add water and cover to steam cabbage for about 15 minutes. Check water level often so it doesn't dry out; add more if needed.

6. Return bacon to the pan and let the cabbage continue to cook for another 5 minutes, uncovered.

6 slices of bacon, chopped

½ medium onion, chopped

2 cloves of garlic, minced

1 large head cabbage, rough sliced

¼ cup apple cider vinegar

1 tsp smoked paprika

½ tsp Korean pepper flakes

Himalayan salt and pepper, to taste

½ cup water

We keep a little of the juices in this dish and add just ¼ tsp of xanthan gum to create a loose sauce to complete the dish.

Jazz this dish up with a drizzle of keto-friendly hot sauce.

carbs	fibre	fat	protein
15.75g	6.25g	12.25g	8g

This recipe has so many possibilities! You can change up the ingredients to make it sweet instead of savoury. Just add a little sweetener (we recommend stevia or erythritol) and omit the onion and cheese, and you've got yourself a base that you can add anything to—keto friendly chocolate chips, a few berries—or just have it on its own. Try the sweet version of these biscuits covered with whipping cream, perfect with a cup of tea.

The savoury biscuits can be dipped into stews, soups, casseroles, or covered with keto-friendly gravy (like our Cream Cheese Gravy, page 215). If you're having Italian, you can add Italian spices and a little Parmesan. For Indian add some garam masala and curry, and for Mexican add chili powder and cumin. Make this recipe your own and give it all the flavours you like.

These biscuits are the perfect thing to serve with Game Day Chili (page 164).

SAVOURY CHEESY BISCUITS

SERVINGS 8   **SERVING SIZE** 1 biscuit

½ cup almond flour

½ cup coconut flour

½ tsp cream of tartar

½ tsp Himalayan pink salt

¼ tsp baking soda

¼ cup sour cream, crème fraîche, or Greek yogurt (not light or fat-free)

2 large eggs

¼ cup green onions, chopped

2 tbsp softened butter, oil, or bacon fat

⅓ cup cheddar, shredded

1. Preheat oven to 350°F.

2. Combine dry ingredients. Set aside.

3. In a separate bowl, mix the sour cream, green onions, eggs, and softened butter.

4. Fold dry ingredients into the wet until mixture is thoroughly combined.

5. Carefully fold in the cheese, being careful not to mix too much.

6. Mould mixture into a flat disc (or individual biscuits) on parchment paper and bake for 20 minutes or until the edge starts to brown.

7. Cut the biscuit into triangle slices and serve.

carbs	fibre	fat	protein
6.75g	3.25g	14.75g	7.75g

We increase the oven temp to 375°F for the last 5 minutes to brown up the biscuit.

Scalloped Radish Casserole is a gratin, one of those comfort dishes that just makes you feel at home. The creamy goodness has perfectly balanced flavours that will fill up your family's tummies in a hurry. They'll be so happy gobbling up this dish that they won't even realize it's not made with potatoes.

Daikon radish is the star of Scalloped Radish Casserole. The long white daikon is sliced thinly, seasoned just right, and combined with cream and spices to bring you a delightfully creamy side dish. Serve it to your guests with some baked ham or a small steak.

SCALLOPED RADISH CASSEROLE

SERVINGS 4   **SERVING SIZE** 1½ cups

1. Boil daikon radish for about 20 minutes. Set aside.

2. Microwave onion for 2 minutes or until translucent.

3. Combine all remaining ingredients except cheddar and paprika in a medium saucepan. Simmer at low-medium for about 10 minutes. Set aside to cool.

4. Layer the ingredients in a casserole dish starting with cheese sauce, then radish, then onion. Repeat.

5. Bake at 375°F for 60 minutes.

6. Remove from oven and sprinkle cheddar and paprika on top.

7. Return to the oven and bake for another 10 minutes, or until cheese is melted.

1	large daikon radish, thinly sliced (about 4 cups)
1	cup onion, thinly sliced
1	cup whipping cream (35%)
1	cup cream cheese
⅛	cup coconut flour
4	tbsp butter
1	tbsp Dijon
1	tsp dried parsley
1	tsp pepper
½	tsp ancho chili, or regular chili powder
½	tsp garlic powder
½	tsp onion powder
½	cup old cheddar, shredded
1	tsp paprika

carbs	fibre	fat	protein
10.5g	4.5g	51g	7g

Zucchini Latkes are a family favourite for us, especially at the end of the summer. We watch our little garden all summer in anticipation of the delectable creations that will come from our labour of love. Anybody who's ever grown zucchini plants knows they produce an abundance of squash, leaving most people wondering what to do with it all after they've made a handful of meals. After all the neighbours are fitted out with gifted offerings, and the pickling and zoodles (spiralled zucchini) are done, we start making our Zucchini Latkes.

Latkes are traditionally made with potatoes; these Zucchini Latkes have all the taste of the old-fashioned kind without the heavy carb load. Our preference is to have a little Keto Mayo (page 227) or other sauce on the side for dipping.

These Zucchini Latkes freeze well, so go ahead and make yourself double and triple batches and store them in your freezer for up to two months.

ZUCCHINI LATKES

SERVINGS 4   **SERVING SIZE** 1 latke

1   cup zucchini, grated, excess moisture removed

2   eggs

½   cup Parmesan, grated

½   cup crème fraîche

⅓   cup green onion (tops only), chopped

2   cloves of garlic, minced

⅛   cup coconut flour

⅛   cup almond flour

1   tbsp fresh basil, shredded (or 1 tsp dry basil)

⅛   tsp thyme

Himalayan pink salt and pepper, to taste

keto-friendly oil, to grease the pan (e.g., extra virgin olive oil, lard, bacon fat)

1. Combine all ingredients and form into four patties. We make ours about 2.5 inches in diameter and about 1 inch thick.

2. Heat oil in a frying pan over medium heat.

3. Sauté patties for 4-5 minutes, then flip.

4. Reduce heat and cook for an additional 4 minutes.

5. Serve immediately.

carbs	fibre	fat	protein
5g	2g	8g	9.5g

Place zucchini on paper towel after grating and squeeze out excess moisture so it doesn't make your fritters soggy.

SAUCES & EXTRAS

Buttery and Rich Pancake Syrup will save your sanity on a Saturday morning. Pancakes are just not the same without syrup. Butter is lovely on pancakes or waffles, and there are some jam type syrups out there that are tasty as well, but there is nothing that replaces the sticky, yummy syrup that we all grew up with.

This Buttery and Rich Pancake Syrup is built around brown butter. Any recipe that calls for regular butter will only be made better by the extra step of browning the butter ahead of time. It's a basic kitchen technique that will take any dish up a notch. Some people separate the brown nutty liquid butter from the residue at the bottom of the pan, but we think it adds to the flavour and the magic of the dish. Those little brown particles literally dance in the liquid, suspended in sweet yumminess.

(Remember, we don't expect our food to taste the same as before keto—it was all those tastes that got us into trouble!)

BUTTERY AND RICH PANCAKE SYRUP

SERVINGS 2   **SERVING SIZE** ¼ cup

3   tbsp butter

1   cup water

¼   cup confectioner's Swerve

1   drop of maple essence or food grade essential oil (We use LorAnn's.)

1   tsp vanilla

1   pinch salt

sprinkle of xanthan gum (optional)

1. Add butter to a frying pan and melt over low-medium heat. Stir or swirl it to make sure it's cooking evenly. Watch the butter carefully to make sure it doesn't burn.

2. Cook the butter at a medium temperature until it transforms from a golden yellow into a rich caramel colour.

3. Add the next three ingredients and bring to a boil for about 5 minutes. You will see the syrup start to reduce and thicken.

4. Remove from heat and stir in vanilla and salt.

carbs	fibre	fat	protein
0g	0g	17.5g	0g

 Use a sprinkle of xanthan gum to thicken this sauce, if desired.

A good Caesar dressing is one of the staples of a keto kitchen. There are many commercial Caesar dressings out there, but none that would suit a clean keto lifestyle.

Thankfully there is no need to go without. This homemade Caesar Dressing is super easy and is also customizable.

We tried so many recipes and found they were too heavy, too bland, or too strong. We decided to use a combination of three oils to get the perfect values of healthy fats and flavour. The amount of fresh garlic in this recipe hits our taste buds with a perfect pungent balance that we just love.

You can decrease or increase the amount of garlic to suit your tastes, and you can also change the amount of Parmesan to increase or decrease the salty umami factor. Whatever way you like it, this bare-bones recipe will be your best friend.

CAESAR DRESSING   **SERVINGS** 10   **SERVING SIZE** 2 tablespoons

1. Blend all ingredients except egg in an immersion blender or Bullet.

2. Add egg and allow it to sink to the bottom of the mixture.

3. Place immersion blender on the bottom, and as the dressing starts to thicken, slowly move it up through the mixture.

4. Use right away or refrigerate for up to a week.

¾   cup olive oil

½   cup Parmesan, grated

¼   cup avocado oil

¼   cup coconut oil

3   tbsp apple cider vinegar

3   tbsp lemon juice

1   tbsp Dijon mustard

4   cloves of garlic, grated

1   tsp fish sauce

Himalayan pink salt and pepper, to taste

1   egg

carbs	fibre	fat	protein
.6g	0g	24g	2g

This is a basic cream cheese frosting that will work on many sweet recipes in your kitchen. We use it on Decadent Brownies (page 292), Carrot Cake (page 287), and many more.

It's delicious in a vanilla flavour but can also be quickly adapted to chocolate or any other flavour to suit your tastes.

 Leave cream cheese and butter out of the fridge to let them come to room temperature. Never heat these ingredients.

CREAM CHEESE FROSTING

SERVINGS 8   **SERVING SIZE** 1 tablespoon

4   oz cream cheese, softened

¼   cup butter, softened

½   cup powdered Swerve or equivalent

½   tsp vanilla extract

1. Cream the butter and cream cheese together with a hand mixer until fully combined.

2. Add the sweetener and vanilla extract and continue to mix.

3. Once the sweetener is blended in, continue to mix until fluffy.

carbs 5g	fibre 0g	fat 10g	protein 1g

 For chocolate icing, add 2 tbsp cocoa.

Icing should be used immediately, but you can store it in an airtight container in the refrigerator for up to a week.

This recipe will be your best friend for so many food situations: Sunday dinner, poutine (such as Jiggs' Dinner Poutine, page 64), meatballs, pork chop dinner. A spoonful of Cream Cheese Gravy will take any of these meals up a notch and add to the comfort food factor as well. This gravy is usually built on a panful of meat drippings after the meat has been removed.

Note that the ingredient amounts will vary greatly. We use ⅛ cup of cream cheese to thicken/flavour gravy for a dinner for two and ½ cup to enhance a turkey dinner. Use these recipe amounts loosely in accordance to your own gravy preferences.

The amount of xanthan gum depends on how thick you like your gravy and how much liquid you have to start. Sprinkle the gum into your liquid until you reach your desired consistency.

CREAM CHEESE GRAVY

meat or bacon drippings

½ cup broth or stock (beef, chicken, or vegetable), per serving

¼ cup cream cheese

1 tbsp coconut sauce

¼ tsp xanthan gum (optional)

Himalayan salt and pepper, to taste

¼ tsp thyme (fresh, if possible)

1. Deglaze pan with broth, then simmer.

2. Add cream cheese and coconut sauce and whisk until smooth.

3. Slowly add in xanthan gum, keeping in mind that it will thicken as it cools.

4. Add thyme, and salt and pepper to taste.

 If making turkey gravy, we usually add garlic, a small carrot, turkey wings, and thyme to the pan as it is deglazing and simmering. This adds to the flavour tenfold.

If you thicken the gravy too much, add extra broth.

Sometimes you need a light and loose cream cheese sauce to ring your sweet treat up a notch. Use this as a warm topping to give a cake-type dessert extra pizzazz.

1   cup cream cheese

¼   cup whipping cream (35%)

1   tbsp erythritol, stevia, or equivalent

1   tsp vanilla

CREAM CHEESE SAUCE

SERVINGS 5   **SERVING SIZE** ¼ cup

1.   Melt cream cheese in a saucepan over low-medium heat. Add sweetener, whipping cream, and vanilla. Whisk to remove all the lumps and set aside. Sauce will thicken as it cools. Reheat if it gets too thick.

carbs	fibre	fat	protein
2g	0g	1.6g	3g

 This Cream Cheese Sauce is also a decadent alternative to our Buttery and Rich Pancake Syrup on pancakes and waffles.

A creamy custard to accompany your keto desserts. Whip up a simple keto cake and layer it with custard and berries for a dessert that is as familiar to many East Coast kitchens as an old-fashioned trifle.

CUSTARD   **SERVINGS** 4   **SERVING SIZE** ¼ cup

1. Combine first three ingredients in a medium saucepan and simmer for 10 minutes.

2. In a separate bowl, whisk eggs and egg yolks.

3. Slowly whisk/incorporate hot liquid into egg (i.e., temper the eggs).

4. Add Swerve.

5. Whisk in xanthan a little bit at a time.

6. Return to a saucepan and cook over medium heat for 5 minutes, stirring constantly.

1	cup cold water
2	tbsp butter
2	oz cream cheese
2	eggs
2	egg yolks (reserve whites for meringue)
1	cup Swerve
½	tsp xanthan gum

carbs	fibre	fat	protein
.75g	0g	18g	8g

A food processor can be used instead of a pastry cutter. Pulse to combine until crumbly, then add eggs and vinegar and pulse again. Dough will be crumbly when finished. Pick up recipe instructions, starting with step 4.

Pastry was a tough one for me to convert. In my pre-keto days, I was known as the queen of pastry among my closer friends. I learned that perfect recipe very young in life, thanks to my grandmother.

It was a bit challenging getting that same texture using keto ingredients. Some of the pastry rules are the same: don't overwork your dough; the heat from your hands isn't good for the dough, so try to work the dough with tools instead. But after that, the rules totally change. Don't get frustrated if you have to attempt this a few times before you get the results you want. It took me a few tries to get the feel for the new ingredients.

The secret is truly keeping the dough cool and learning to work fast. The more you fool with the dough, the tougher it will get.

ECK PIE CRUST   SERVINGS 1 pie crust

½   cup almond flour

¼   cup confectioner's Swerve

⅛   cup coconut flour

½   tsp xanthan gum

¼   tsp Himalayan pink salt

½   cup cold butter, cut into small chunks

¼   cup cold cream cheese, cut into small chunks

1   egg, whisked

2   tsp vinegar

coconut flour for dusting the parchment

1. In one bowl, combine the flours, Swerve, xanthan gum, and salt and set aside.

2. In a second, bigger bowl, combine butter and cream cheese with a pastry cutter. (For food processor, see note above.)

3. Add in egg and vinegar and combine again with the cutter.

4. Wrap dough in plastic wrap, transfer to the fridge, and let rest for 1 hour to 3 days.

5. Sprinkle a very thin layer of coconut flour on your rolling surface and roll out the dough between two sheets of parchment.

6. Place the dough back in the fridge for 10-15 minutes to cool it down again. This will prevent the dough from sticking to the parchment.

7. Remove from fridge and gently peel off one layer of parchment. Lay the crust into a pie plate and remove top layer of parchment.

For a savoury crust, omit the Swerve.

CONTINUES ▶

carbs	fibre	fat	protein
22g	11g	145g	25g

Values are for the entire crust. Adjust macros based on the size of your slice(s).

8. Leaving about 1 inch of extra dough all the way around, cut the extra dough from the outside edge of your pie plate. Tuck the inch of dough under, creating a double layer on the outer edge of your pie crust.

9. Use one finger to push the pastry down toward the outside of the dish. Using the finger and thumb of your other hand, pinch around that finger to create a scalloped effect.

10. Bake at 350°F for 15-20 minutes, or until the crust is a light golden brown. Time is dependent on the size of your crust—shorter times for tarts or turnovers, longer for large pies.

 Cover edges of the pie crust with aluminum foil if the outer edges start to burn.

Our Guacamole goes hand in hand with our Salsa Chicken (page 179), Game Day Chili (page 164), or any other dish that has a spicy flavour profile. Scoop it up with some Keto Cheesy Crackers (page 224) or pork rinds for a late-night keto indulgence. Guacamole is always best when it's fresh, but it may be stored in the fridge in a sealed container.

GUACAMOLE

SERVINGS 2   **SERVING SIZE** ⅓ cup (depending on the size of the avocado)

1. Cut the avocado in half and remove the seed. Scoop out the flesh and place it into a medium-sized bowl.

2. Add the lime juice, garlic, salt, and pepper and gently mash the avocado and incorporate all ingredients.

1   ripe avocado

½   tbsp lime juice

1   clove of garlic, minced

Himalayan pink salt and pepper

OPTIONAL ADDITIONS
¼ cup chopped tomato | ¼ cup chopped onion | ⅛ cup fresh chopped cilantro | ⅛ cup crumbled bacon

 Press plastic wrap into the guacamole with your fingers before sealing any leftovers. It will help keep the avocado from oxidizing and turning colour.

carbs	fibre	fat	protein
0g	5.5g	10.5g	1.5g

We're billing this one as a holiday stuffing for a turkey dinner, but it can also be used for a Sunday chicken dinner or a good old plate of NL chips with dressing and gravy.

Oh. Yes. You. CAN!

CDG (short for chips, dressing, and gravy), as it's affectionately called in many NL homes, is probably one of the bigger reasons that I got myself overweight and unhealthy in the first place, as the pre-keto version is really a plate of carbs, loaded with more carbs. This keto Holiday Dressing will allow you to have your CDG and eat it too, without guilt.

Throw the dressing atop some daikon or jicama fried with some cream cheese gravy and you're in business.

Enjoy!

HOLIDAY DRESSING

SERVINGS 4   **SERVING SIZE** ½ cup

Two-Minute Microwave Bread (page 250)

⅓ medium onion, minced

¼ cup butter, melted

summer savoury, to taste

salt and pepper, to taste

1. Make Two-Minute Microwave Bread and chop it into 1-inch pieces.

2. Place onion and butter in a microwave-safe dish and cook for 1 minute or until onion is translucent. Set aside to cool.

3. Add savoury, salt, and pepper (to taste) to the bread pieces, then pile them on two sheets of tinfoil, criss-crossed in an X. Toss to combine.

4. Add slightly cooled butter/onion combination to the crumbs and combine with your hands, making sure to press the butter into all the crumbs.

5. Fold the tinfoil over to create a foil packet full of dressing.

6. About 30 or 40 minutes before serving dinner, place the tinfoil packet on the rack in the oven.

7. Remove from oven, open packet, and serve.

carbs	fibre	fat	protein
7.5g	2g	27g	4g

Have you noticed how hard it is to find a great keto sausage? We searched high and low and got very frustrated, so we changed tactics and put the effort into researching how to make our own. We found that the secret ingredient in sausage is fennel seed. Buy the seeds and either crush or grind them up with a mortar and pestle. Either way, don't leave the fennel out of the recipe—it's really the star of the show.

HOMEMADE SAUSAGE MIX

SERVINGS 4   **SERVING SIZE** 2 oz

1. Add all ingredients to a mixing bowl and gently combine, then fry until golden brown.

½	lb ground pork
1	egg
3	cloves of garlic, minced
2	tbsp bacon fat
1	tbsp flax meal
1	tsp onion powder
1	tsp paprika
½	tsp cumin
½	tsp fennel seed, crushed
½	tsp salt

carbs	fibre	fat	protein
2.5g	1g	20g	11g

Sometimes you just need a good, old-fashioned cracker. It might be for spreading a thick coating of soft goat cheese, or company's coming and you're making fancy hors d'eouvres (horses dovers, we call them), or maybe you just need something to dip into our amazing Onion Dip (page 235). Keto Cheesy Crackers to the rescue! We change out the herbs in this recipe to suit the application. They're all delightful.

KETO CHEESY CRACKERS

SERVINGS 4   **SERVING SIZE** 7 to 10 crackers

½ cup almond flour

½ tsp garlic powder

½ tsp onion powder

½ tsp sea salt

½ tsp cream of tartar

¼ tsp baking soda

¼ tsp rosemary, oregano, dill, basil, or thyme (your choice)

1   egg

½ cup cheese, grated (We use old cheddar.)

¼ cup cream cheese

1   tbsp extra virgin olive oil

1. Preheat oven to 350°F.

2. Combine all dry ingredients in a medium bowl.

3. Whisk the egg, cheeses, and extra virgin olive oil in a separate bowl.

4. Combine wet and dry ingredients with a spatula or wooden spoon. Form the dough into a ball and place it on a large piece of parchment paper on the counter. Add another equivalent sized piece to the top of your dough ball and then slightly flatten the dough ball between the sheets with your hands.

5. Roll out the dough with a rolling pin until the dough is even and reaches the thickness of your desired cracker.

6. Using a sharp knife or pizza cutter, gently score the crackers into squares or triangles.

7. Transfer the parchment-covered dough to a baking sheet.

8. Bake for 15-18 minutes.

9. Remove from the oven and let cool for 5 minutes.

10. Break up the crackers using the scored lines, then scatter them on the baking sheet and return them to the oven for an additional 5 minutes.

11. Cool before enjoying.

12. Store in a sealed container in the fridge.

carbs 4.5g	fibre 1.5g	fat 26g	protein 6.5g

 For a lower carb value, these crackers can be made without the almond flour.

Keto Mayonnaise is a delightfully light homemade mayo that serves well as a sandwich spread or as the basis of a great salad dressing. Like many of our keto recipes, this one took many attempts before we reached the perfect blend of oils. We use farm-fresh eggs when making our Keto Mayonnaise, but eggs from the store will do as well.

Keto Mayonnaise will quickly become your family's favourite condiment. You can feel confident serving it at your family get-togethers and backyard barbecues, knowing you are serving a sauce made with healthy fats, eggs, and other clean ingredients. No more worries about what's lurking in the jar in the refrigerator. Make this recipe and enjoy! It's okay to indulge sometimes.

KETO MAYONNAISE

SERVINGS 17   **SERVING SIZE** 1 tablespoon

1. Place all ingredients into the cylinder of an immersion blender, allowing the egg to sink to the bottom.
2. Place the immersion blender on the bottom and slowly raise it from the bottom to the top. You will see the texture of the ingredients change as they become mayonnaise.
3. Use immediately or store in your refrigerator for up to one week.

⅓ cup coconut oil

⅓ cup avocado oil

¼ cup extra light olive oil

1 large egg

1½ tsp Dijon mustard

1 tsp apple cider vinegar

1 tsp lemon juice

½ tsp Himalayan pink salt

 Feel free to tweak Keto Mayonnaise for the flavours that suit your family best.

carbs	fibre	fat	protein
0g	0g	12g	.5g

We know it's not the same as the ketchup you've eaten all your life, but that ketchup, usually filled with sugar, is one of those things that got us into trouble in the first place, isn't it?

Kwick Keto Ketchup is best served warm. I know! That's not what you're used to either, but I promise you're gonna love it.

Dollop a spoonful on top of your next burger, or cozy a little next to your keto fries. Welcome to the world of warm keto ketchup! There is no end to the places you will learn to love this condiment.

PS: It's just as lovely served cold.

KWICK KETO KETCHUP

SERVINGS 64   **SERVING SIZE** 2 tablespoons

¼   cup olive oil

½   can (28 oz) of San Marzano tomatoes

⅛   cup apple cider vinegar

1   tbsp coconut sauce

¼   cup confectioner's Swerve (or equivalent)

1   tbsp Dijon mustard

1   tsp garlic powder

1   tsp onion powder

1   tsp oregano

1   tsp paprika (We use smoked.)

1.   Heat extra virgin olive oil in a deep sauté pan over medium heat.

2.   Add tomatoes, apple cider vinegar, and coconut sauce. Simmer for 10 minutes, then remove from heat.

3.   Allow to cool slightly, then use an immersion blender (or transfer the stewed tomatoes to a blender or Bullet). Whiz up the contents of the pan until all the tomato pieces are blended into a thick sauce.

4.   Add remaining ingredients and simmer for 10 minutes.

5.   Use immediately, served warm, or store in the fridge in a sealed container for up to 1 week.

carbs .7g	fibre .15g	fat .8g	protein .1g

To elevate this ketchup, use diced tomatoes in place of the canned. Heat the ingredients just enough to slightly warm the fresh tomatoes.

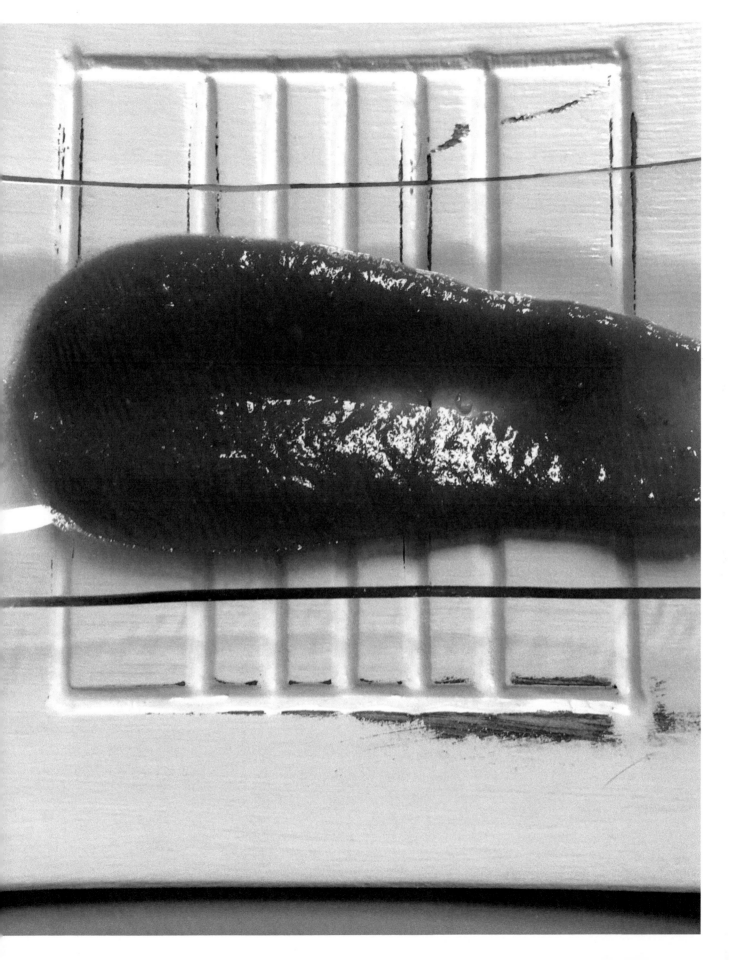

Our homemade Lemon Curd can be the star of lemon meringue pie, a filling for cakes, or a spread for keto biscuits and scones.

Except for the addition of lemon and Step 1, this Lemon Curd recipe is the same as the one for Custard (page 217). It can be made several days in advance and stored in the fridge.

LEMON CURD   SERVINGS 4   SERVING SIZE ¼ cup

1. Combine first 4 ingredients in a medium saucepan and bring to a boil then, remove from the heat right away. Don't let this reduce, as it will throw off the proper balance of ingredients.

2. Follow steps 2-6 of the Custard recipe, page 217.

1   cup cold water

2   tbsp butter

2   oz cream cheese

juice and zest of 1 lemon

2   eggs

2   egg yolks (preserve whites for meringue)

1   cup Swerve

½   tsp xanthan gum

carbs	fibre	fat	protein
1.5g	0g	18g	8g

A well-rounded and multitalented tomato sauce, this simple marinara can be personalized with extra spices or veggies and used in many Italian dishes. It's great with a bowl of zoodles (zucchini noodles) or spaghetti squash and meatballs.

This recipe, like many others here, is a combination of both of our recipes—Hubby's and mine—and then ketofied. Although tomatoes are higher in carb values, they are acceptable in moderation after you're fat adapted. As long as you don't fill your plate to overflowing, you should be fine with this Meatless Marinara Sauce. Just make sure you factor it into your daily carb expenditure.

2	tbsp extra virgin olive oil or bacon fat
1	onion, chopped
3	cloves of garlic, minced
1	tsp dried oregano
1	tsp dried parsley
½	tsp dried basil
½	tsp red pepper flakes
½	tsp rosemary
1	can (28 oz) San Marzano tomatoes
2	tbsp red wine vinegar
1	tsp Parmesan, grated

Himalayan salt and pepper, to taste

MEATLESS MARINARA SAUCE

SERVINGS 7   **SERVING SIZE** ½ cup

1. Heat extra virgin olive oil in a saucepan over medium heat and sauté onion until translucent.

2. Add garlic and continue to cook for 3 minutes.

3. Push onion and garlic to the sides of the pan and add the herbs and spices, one by one, right into the oil. Then combine with the onions and garlic and reduce to a simmer.

4. Purée the tomatoes in an immersion blender or Bullet then add them to the mixture.

5. Stir in the remaining ingredients and simmer for at least 15 minutes.

carbs 3.5g	fibre .5g	fat 4g	protein 1g

 Real onion and garlic is our preference for this recipe, but dehydrated versions may be used, in which case substitute 1 tsp of garlic and onion powder and add them to the listed spices.

Onion Dip is not an everyday indulgence. Although available year-round, it was only at Christmastime that chip dips would make an appearance in grocery stores where we grew up.

For me, this dip brings back memories of family and of visiting friends. Of crispy, salty snacks, great conversation, and letting the good times roll.

Our Onion Dip is great for veggie platters and also for movie night with a loved one and a bowl of Keto Cheesy Crackers (page 224) or pork rinds.

ONION DIP

SERVINGS 4   **SERVING SIZE** ⅓ cup

1. Combine all ingredients and serve.

1	cup crème fraîche
2	oz cream cheese
1	tbsp minced dried onion
1	tsp onion powder
1	tsp parsley
½	tsp garlic powder
¼	tsp Himalayan pink salt

carbs	fibre	fat	protein
2.25g	.25g	28g	2.5g

We use this sauce as a topping for Bacon-Wrapped Baked Brie (page 50), pancakes, our Old-fashioned Jam Jams (page 304), cheesecake, or our Savoury Cheesy Biscuits (page 200). Add a half cup of vinegar to turn it into a gastrique. What's a gastrique, you ask? Well, it's a fancy name for a sweet and sour sauce.

PARTRIDGEBERRY SAUCE/GASTRIQUE

SERVINGS 4   **SERVING SIZE** ¼ cup

1   cup partridgeberries

½   cup Swerve

½   tsp salt

½   cup vinegar (only for gastrique)

1. Combine all ingredients in a small saucepan and simmer for 5 minutes.

carbs	fibre	fat	protein
3.25g	1.25g	0g	0g

Perfectly Pickled Chanterelles are made with in-season chanterelle mushrooms, but any type of edible mushroom can be used. Take care when foraging for your own mushrooms, and never eat any wild plant unless you're absolutely certain of its identification.

These delightful, meaty, apricot-coloured mushrooms begin to pop up in late May, and we have a bounty of them right up until October. We like to help Mother Nature extend the season a little bit, so as soon as we've had our first bellyful of these tasty mushrooms, we start putting them away. We dry some and freeze some, but by far our favourite way to put them aside is to pickle them. Perfectly Pickled Chanterelles will dress up any charcuterie board and add a zesty side to a steak. Try throwing a handful on some keto toast for a delightful snack.

PERFECTLY PICKLED CHANTERELLES

SERVINGS 16   **SERVING SIZE** ¼ cup

1. Clean your chanterelles by cutting/scraping away any damaged, dirty, or bruised portions and trimming off any damaged stems. Dry fry them whole in a large frying pan. When the chanterelles have given up most of their water, remove them from the pan. Set aside.

2. Add a portion of each of the jar ingredients to each jar. You may increase or decrease these amounts according to your own tastes.

3. Put all the pickle juice ingredients into the mushroom pan and bring to a boil to deglaze the pan.

4. Turn the temperature down to a simmer and cook for 5 minutes. Turn off the heat.

5. Pack the mushrooms firmly into jars, leaving half-inch headspace.

6. Spoon the pickle juice into each jar. Add more pickling vinegar to top off each jar and bring the liquid to within a quarter inch of the rim, making certain that the liquid completely covers the mushrooms.

7. Boil the sealed jars for 15 minutes to complete the canning/sterilization process.

1-1½ lbs chanterelles or other mushrooms

canning jars with lids and rings (3 or 4 if using 8 oz jars)

IN EACH JAR, PUT

bell peppers, sliced

onion, sliced

garlic, sliced

2   tbsp mustard seed

1   bay leaf

1   sprig thyme

pinch allspice

pinch coriander

pinch red pepper flakes

FOR THE PICKLE JUICE

1½   cups white pickling vinegar

½   cup dry white wine

½   cup water

3   tbsp apple cider vinegar

2   tbsp Himalayan pink salt

carbs	fibre	fat	protein
2.5g	1.25g	0g	.5g

One of the first ketofied meals we tried was pizza. We had done our research and decided that "fat head crust" was the one for us. Chicken or cauliflower crust just wasn't going to satisfy our tastes, being the foodies that we are. We were so excited! We had seen so many posts about this fat head pizza crust with fellow ketonians raving about how good it was. We were on a keto way of eating and were still getting to have pizza? Incredible!

We mixed up our dough, baked it, topped it, and waited. It smelled incredible. We were literally drooling. As soon as it was cooked, we popped it out of the oven and served it up. We were so looking forward our pizza that it's a wonder we didn't burn the mouths off ourselves with the hot cheese.

It was okay. Not amazing, just okay. The bigger issue was that within five minutes of eating a slice, we felt like the crust was made of lead and was weighing down in our stomachs and making us feel bloated. Fat head wasn't the one for us.

We took it upon ourselves to create a pizza crust that has the right taste and texture but not the heavy almond flour. When we finally created this Pizza Crust, we were amazed at how much we liked it. I remember the first time we tried it. Hubby and I looked at each other and both said at the same time "OMG, this is pizza!" No bloating, no aftertaste, and no cheating. Win, win, win! Hope you enjoy it too.

Pizza mozzarella is a blend of two cheeses with a lower moisture content than regular mozzarella. Better for browning, melting, and grating.

Add ¼ cup almond flour to make the crust denser.

PIZZA CRUST

SERVINGS 8   **SERVING SIZE** 1 slice

2   cups pizza mozzarella, shredded

1   egg

garlic powder, to taste

½   tsp oregano (optional)

1. Combine all ingredients and press onto a parchment-covered pizza pan.

2. Bake at 350°F for 10 minutes, then cover with another sheet of parchment to flip it. Cook for another 10 minutes.

3. Flip once more and cook for the last 10 minutes.

Press the crust so that the edges are slightly thicker, to create a more finished look.

Top this crust with garlic butter and 1 tsp parsley for a delicious keto garlic bread.

carbs	fibre	fat	protein
1g	0g	5.5g	7.5g

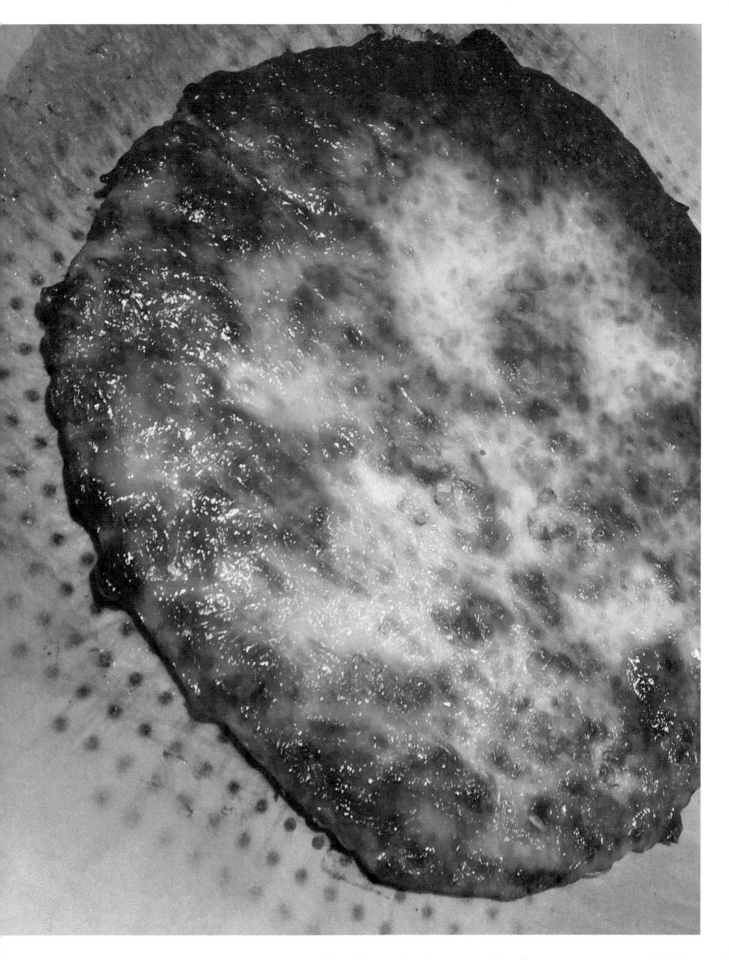

Russian Salad Dressing is our go-to for a tangy yet sweet sauce for a salad. The celery seeds add a pop of crunch and a distinct warm, earthy celery taste.

RUSSIAN SALAD DRESSING

SERVINGS 16　　**SERVING SIZE** ¼ cup

1	cup coconut oil
½	cup tomato paste
¼	cup confectioner's Swerve
¼	cup minced onion flakes
2-3	tbsp lemon juice
1½	tsp celery seeds
1	tsp coconut sauce
1	tsp fish sauce
1	tsp garlic powder
1	tsp vinegar
½	tsp paprika
½	tsp salt
½	tsp thyme

1. Combine all ingredients and enjoy on your next salad.

We combine ours in a Mason jar with a tight lid. A couple of good shakes gives it the perfect mix.

carbs	fibre	fat	protein
1.6g	.4g	28g	.5g

One might think this salsa was named after the amount of sauce in this recipe, but in fact it's named after the gent who inspired the recipe. You guessed it, it's a tongue-in-cheek hats off to dear Sidekick Geoff.

This is not only a family favourite, it's also a multitalented recipe. We use it to spice up our breakfast eggs and boost the flavour of our Salsa Chicken (page 179). It can also be added to burgers, pork, or any other food that needs an added kick. The addition of Keto Cheesy Crackers (page 224) or pork rinds turns it into a great movie-night snack.

SAUCY SALSA

SERVINGS 32   **SERVING SIZE** ¼ cup

1   can (28 oz) San Marzano tomatoes, chopped into 1-inch cubes

1   medium onion, chopped

1   cup bell peppers, chopped

2   large jalapeno peppers, seeded and finely chopped

hot peppers to taste (We use 2 Thai chilies.)

¼   cup cider vinegar

⅛   cup Swerve or equivalent

1   tbsp cumin

1   tsp coriander

1   tsp Himalayan pink salt

1.   Put all ingredients into a large pot. Stir well and bring to a boil. Reduce heat and simmer for about 30 minutes, then enjoy.

 The amounts can easily be multiplied for larger batches for canning.

Add a package of cream cheese to 8 ounces of salsa to create a dip for parties or gatherings.

carbs 2.5g	fibre 1g	fat 0g	protein 1g

 We use Thai chilies, but any hot peppers—habanero, Scotch bonnet, serrano, or even ghost (if you dare)—will do, depending on how hot you like your salsa.

This is a full-flavour BBQ sauce for the keto or low-carb household.

The Swerve adds to the caramelization of the sauce. Any other sweetener would have the same taste, but the consistency would not be the same.

Use Smokin' BBQ Sauce on steak, pork, chicken, or anywhere you would use a bold grilling sauce.

SMOKIN' BBQ SAUCE

SERVINGS 32 (32 oz total, 64 tbsp)   **SERVING SIZE** 2 tablespoons

1	can (28 oz) San Marzano tomatoes, pureed
¼	cup confectioner's Swerve
2	tbsp coconut sauce
1	tbsp garlic powder
1	tbsp liquid smoke
1	tbsp onion powder
1	tbsp smoked paprika
½	tbsp cumin
2	tsp dry mustard
1	tsp chili powder
1	tsp salt
1	tsp yellow mustard
½	tsp pepper
½	tsp xanthan gum

1. Combine all ingredients in a medium saucepan and simmer for 5 minutes.

carbs	fibre	fat	protein
1.8g	.3g	0g	1.8g

Sometimes you have a perfect flavour profile on a dish, but you just need to kick the heat up a notch. This is the perfect sauce to rise to the occasion. We use it on BBQ shrimp, grilled chicken, and other spicy offerings. Easy does it on this one—it's a matter of "a little dab will do ya." This recipe makes about 1½ cups.

SWEET THAI CHILI SAUCE

SERVINGS 6   **SERVING SIZE** ¼ cup

1. Combine all ingredients in a medium saucepan and simmer for 20 minutes.

2. Store in the refrigerator for up to 1 week.

1	cup water
½	cup apple cider vinegar
½	cup Swerve
5	cloves of garlic, finely chopped
1	tbsp coconut sauce
½	tbsp Korean pepper flakes
¼	tbsp red pepper flakes
2	tsp sesame oil
1	tsp xanthan gum
¼	tsp cayenne pepper

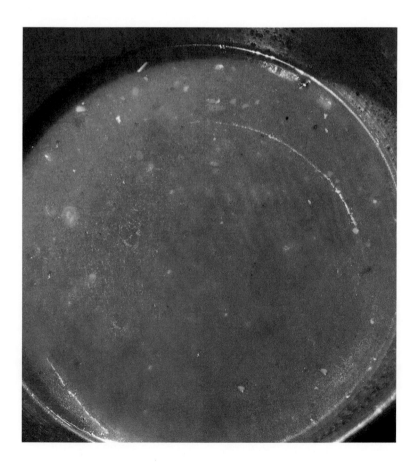

carbs	fibre	fat	protein
2g	.5g	1g	0g

Tastes Like Real Bread Keto Bread was a real challenge for us. We tried so many recipes and they all came up short—it was like Goldilocks and the Three Bears. Only instead of the porridge being too hot/too cold, ours were too eggy, too grainy, and plain old ugh, just not right.

So, as is often the case in the East Coast Keto test kitchen, we took it upon ourselves to create that perfect recipe. I have to admit, it took us a few tries to get it right, and Sidekick Geoff happily sacrificed himself to taste-test every one.

It seems the one thing ketonians miss the most is that good ole slice of bread. We think our Tastes like Real Bread Keto Bread fits the bill and ticks off all the boxes. And the bonus is that your kitchen will smell like Nan's did, way back when.

TASTES LIKE REAL BREAD KETO BREAD

SERVINGS 10   **SERVING SIZE** 1 slice

1. Preheat oven to 350°F.

2. Add cream of tartar to the egg whites and beat them until very stiff peaks form. Set aside.

3. Mix the remaining dry ingredients in a large bowl.

4. Add the water, vinegar, and egg yolks to the dry ingredients while beating with a hand mixer for about 60 seconds. Make sure you take time to allow the dry ingredients to absorb the liquid.

5. With a spatula, fold the egg whites into the mixture, being careful not to break the meringue. (You just fluffed air into those egg whites; over mixing will deflate them and not allow your bread to be as fluffy. The aerated eggs [meringue] will give your bread lift.)

6. Spoon into a loaf pan and tamp the pan down once or twice to let the air bubbles settle.

7. Using a spatula, pull extra dough into the centre of the loaf, forming a traditional loaf shape. Bread will rise slightly, but you have to form the centre rise yourself.

8. Bake on middle oven rack for 15 minutes, then turn your oven down to 325°F and bake for 50-60 minutes, depending on the size of your bread. It's done when you hear a hollow sound when tapping the bottom of the loaf.

6	egg whites
¼	tsp cream of tartar
⅓	cup super fine almond flour
4	tbsp psyllium husks
1	tbsp nutritional yeast
1	tsp active instant yeast
1	tsp sea salt
1	cup lukewarm water
2	tsp cider vinegar
4	egg yolks

carbs	fibre	fat	protein
5.4g	1.7g	9.3g	6.7g

Sometimes you want a slice of keto bread and you don't have time to bake a full loaf. Two-Minute Microwave Bread to the rescue!

This recipe can be pressed into service as a quick burger bun, a sandwich for lunch, or as the base for our Holiday Dressing (page 220). We like it best toasted or fried in bacon fat to make it extra crisp and give it a boost of flavour.

TWO-MINUTE MICROWAVE BREAD

SERVINGS 1   **SERVING SIZE** 2 slices

1	egg
3	tsp almond flour
1	tbsp butter, melted
½	tsp baking soda
⅛	tsp cream of tartar

1. Combine all ingredients in a mug or microwave-safe plastic container. Microwave for 90 seconds. Let cool and slice in half.

carbs	fibre	fat	protein
5g	2g	27g	11g

 Dry fry in a frying pan to toast the bread.

Our White Balsamic Vinaigrette is a light, bright salad dressing that pairs well with a side salad to accompany grilled meats or fish or to go alongside a bunless burger. It also makes a great marinade if you're getting a head start on tomorrow's meat dish.

We recommend using white balsamic because it has lower sugars than the darker variety, but it could be substituted with apple cider vinegar. The dressing is 3:1 oil to vinegar.

Layer sliced tomato, buffalo mozzarella, and crushed basil leaves onto a plate. Top with fresh cracked pepper and White Balsamic Vinaigrette. Perfection!

WHITE BALSAMIC VINAIGRETTE

SERVINGS 160 **SERVING SIZE** ⅛ cup

1. Combine all ingredients and serve. May be stored in the refrigerator for up to a week

⅓	cup white balsamic vinegar
½	cup avocado oil
½	cup coconut oil
¼	cup coconut sauce
3	tbsp mustard (Dijon or regular)
1	tsp garlic powder
½	tsp onion powder
½	tsp Himalayan pink salt
½	tsp thyme

Make the vinaigrette in a container with a lid. Combine all ingredients, cover with the lid, and shake vigorously.

carbs	fibre	fat	protein
1g	0g	14g	.2g

Many people in the keto/low-carb world have difficulty reaching their macros, in particular their fat levels. While we don't recommend that you eat fat just to increase your macros, consuming dietary fats will keep you feeling full and satisfied. The following recipes offer scrumptious ways to add in a snack if you're hungry and increase your fat macros at the same time.

FAT BOMBS

BASIC FAT BOMB

1 **FIND YOUR FAT CARRIER.**

Almost all fat bombs require a fat base that will solidify when it is refrigerated and stay solid at room temperature (softening is fine). The most commonly used and reliable fat bases are butter and coconut oil.

FAT BASES: butter | coconut cream | coconut oil | cream cheese | ghee | tree nut cheese (e.g., cashew cheese)

2 **CHOOSE YOUR PERSONAL FLAVOUR FAVES.**

Here's a list of possible ingredients to consider. This list is just a few ideas to get you started. The flavour combinations don't stop there—you can add many types of ingredients. Use your imagination and your palate to guide you to fat bomb heaven.

SWEET: almond butter | berries (blackberries, blueberries, partridgeberries, raspberries, strawberries) | cheese | cinnamon | cocoa powder | coconut cream | flavour essences (i.e., oils) | lemon juice and/or zest | lime juice and/or zest | nuts | peanut butter | sour cream | vanilla | whipping cream (35%)

SAVOURY: bacon bits | chicken | chopped cooked meat (e.g., salami, salmon, steak) | chopped herbs | eggs | ham | lemon/lime zest | low-carb vegetables (like scallions or peppers)

3 **TAKE YOUR FAT BASE AND YOUR DELICIOUS KETOGENIC INGREDIENTS AND PUT THEM ALL TOGETHER INTO ONE DELICIOUS BALL OR BAR.**

To do this, you can either melt or soften your fat base and blend or mix in your ingredients. The melted fat base can be transferred into a container, tray, or plate and refrigerated until it is solid. The softened fat base can be formed into balls or bars (whatever shape you prefer for eating) and refrigerated.

Bacon Cheeseburger Bombs are the serious and savoury cousin of all those ooey gooey, sweet, cream cheese filled, fun fat bombs.

It may be hard to believe, but not everybody has a sweet tooth and those savoury loving ketonians need to hit their fat macros too! Bacon Cheeseburger Bombs still have an ooey gooey cheesy centre, but this bomb full of taste is best dipped in mustard or Smokin' BBQ Sauce (page 246).

BACON CHEESEBURGER BOMBS

SERVINGS 12   **SERVING SIZE** 1 meatball

Homemade Sausage Mix (page 223)

12   pieces cheddar cheese, ½ inch square

12   slices of bacon

1. Preheat oven to 350°F.

2. Divide sausage meat and form into 12 small, flat discs.

3. Place a cube of cheese in the middle of each disc and use your hands to form the disc into a ball, shaped around the cheese. Careful not to squeeze too hard; the more you work the meat the tougher the end product will be.

4. Wrap a strip of bacon around each ball, weaving the bacon so the ball is completely covered (see photo).

5. Place meatballs on a baking sheet and bake for 45 minutes or until cooked thoroughly.

carbs	fibre	fat	protein
.7g	.25g	17g	7g

Blackberries are chock full of flavour all on their own, but the addition of amaretto oil brings the flavour profile to a whole new level.

Blackberries can be switched out for raspberries or strawberries in this fat bomb recipe. Why not try all three?

BLACKBERRY AMARETTO BOMBS

SERVINGS 12   **SERVING SIZE** 1 bomb

1. Melt butter in a small saucepan over medium heat.

2. Add whipping cream and cream cheese. Whisk until smooth.

3. Add sweetener and stir constantly, adjusting to taste.

4. Turn off heat and stir in vanilla, oil, and salt. Blend well.

5. Gently mix in the blackberries.

6. Pour into paper liners in a silicon mini muffin tray and freeze for at least 1 hour.

7. Keep refrigerated.

2	tbsp butter
¼	cup whipping cream (35%)
4	oz cream cheese
¼	cup sweetener (we use Swerve), or to taste
1	tsp vanilla
2-3	drops amaretto oil (We use LorAnn super concentrated oils.)
⅛	tsp salt
6	blackberries, chopped finely

carbs	fibre	fat	protein
1.4g	.2g	5.3g	.75g

This keto fudge is honestly to die for. It's so rich and creamy, it's hard to believe that this is not only a keto-approved food, but it's also good for you! The hardest part of the whole recipe is waiting four hours for it to set.

BLACKBERRY/BLUEBERRY FUDGE BOMBS

SERVINGS 8   **SERVING SIZE** 1 bomb

2	tbsp butter
½	cup whipping cream (35%)
4	oz cream cheese
3	drops Stur Liquid Water Enhancer, berry flavour (or alternative keto water flavouring)
1	tbsp coconut oil
⅛	tsp salt
4	blackberries, minced

1. Melt butter in a small saucepan over medium heat.
2. Add whipping cream and cream cheese. Whisk until smooth.
3. Add flavouring, adjust for taste.
4. Add coconut oil and salt.
5. Heat until bubbling, stirring constantly.
6. Reduce heat and stir in berries. Blend well.
7. Pour into paper liners in a silicon mini muffin tray and refrigerate for 3-4 hours to set.
8. Keep refrigerated.

carbs	fibre	fat	protein
2g	.1g	12g	1.4g

Make sure to check the ingredients of your water enhancer. Many brands use hidden sugars. Buyer beware.

One of the keys to ketogenic living is being prepared and having the proper foods on hand for when you're hungry. These Breakfast Egg Bites were an early addition to our keto game. We kept a steady supply on hand at all times. They were also a staple in Geoff's lunch bag for his work day. It made breaking his fast an easy process. His recommendation is to put them in the microwave in their container and bring them back to your desk to pop in your mouth as you work. No fuss, no mess.

 This recipe is a great one to customize. You can switch out the ingredients for whatever flavour profile, meats, and veggies you prefer.

BREAKFAST EGG BITES

SERVINGS 24   **SERVING SIZE** 2 bites

1. Preheat oven to 350°F.

2. In a medium bowl, whisk together eggs and whipping cream until smooth.

3. Add the crème fraîche, cream of tartar, spices, salt, and pepper, and mix well.

4. Arrange peppers, cheddar, and meat into a mini muffin tray. (We use silicon as they make for an easier removal.)

5. Spoon in egg mixture until muffin cups are about three-quarters full.

6. Place an ovenproof bowl full of water on the oven rack alongside the egg bites to help with their texture and moisture level.

7. Bake for 15-20 minutes, or until the centre has a very slight jiggle.

6   eggs

½   cup whipping cream (35%)

¼   cup crème fraîche, sour cream, or cream cheese

½   tsp cream of tartar

¼   tsp cumin

¼   tsp salt

¼   tsp thyme

pepper to taste

1   cup bell peppers, finely chopped

1   cup cheddar, grated or cubed small

1   cup Homemade Sausage Mix (page 223) or bacon, precooked and chopped into small pieces

 Serve with a dollop of Saucy Salsa (page 244) on the side.

carbs	fibre	fat	protein
1g	.25g	15.25g	5.8g

Thick, indulgent fudge that's intensified by the addition of the dark cherries. We recommend you freeze this fudge into individual size servings, otherwise you may not be able to stop yourself from having one too many pieces.

CHERRY FUDGE BOMBS

SERVINGS 24   **SERVING SIZE** 1 bomb

1	cup cream cheese
½	cup confectioner's Swerve (or to taste)
⅓	cup coconut oil
3	oz unsweetened baking chocolate
1	tsp almond extract
½	tsp vanilla extract
¾	cup dark cherries, chopped

1. Mix all ingredients except cherries.
2. Pat cherries dry on a paper towel.
3. Spoon ½ tsp of cherry into each paper liner in your mini muffin or silicon baking pan. Top up each liner with the remaining cherry mixture.
4. Cover the cherry with the chocolate mix.
5. Freeze for at least 1 hour.
6. Store in the fridge.

carbs	fibre	fat	protein
2.5g	.75g	8g	1.2g

 We spread the cherry over the bottom of the liner so you can have a bit of cherry in every bite.

Chocolate Chip Cookie Dough Bombs are the one fat bomb treat that you won't be able to resist. In fact, we recommend you store them in a sealed container in the freezer if you have an issue with overindulging.

The pre-keto version of these treats was often a roll of the quality dice, especially if you were dealing with ingredients such as raw eggs, but these nuggets of delight will keep your fat macros where they need to be and your tummy happy as well!

Our initial batch of Chocolate Chip Cookie Dough Bombs was made with MCT oil instead of coconut oil, but we found the MCT oil resulted in a bit of an irritated throat for some of our testers, so we switched our recipe back to regular coconut oil. If you don't have crème fraîche, sour cream can be substituted, but the carb value will be increased and the end product will not be as clean. The coconut flour helps to add the "dough feel" to the Chocolate Chip Cookie Dough Bombs. It's not an integral part of the recipe and may be skipped if you don't like the texture it adds.

The nutritional info for these Chocolate Chip Cookie Dough Bombs really depends on how big you make them. We used a mini ice cream scoop, and the bombs were a perfect size. They were one bite for hubby Geoff, while I chose to nibble and usually got three bites per bomb.

CHOCOLATE CHIP COOKIE DOUGH BOMBS

SERVINGS 12   **SERVING SIZE** 1 bomb

1. Combine all ingredients except chocolate with a hand mixer or a whisk.

2. When fully combined, use a spatula to integrate the chocolate chip pieces.

3. Spoon batter onto a wax-paper-lined sheet and refrigerate for 1 hour.

⅓ cup butter, softened

8 oz cream cheese, softened

½ cup crème fraîche or sour cream

¼ cup coconut oil

¼ cup confectioner's Swerve

1 tbsp coconut flour

2 tsp vanilla extract

pinch Himalayan pink salt

¼ cup sugar-free chocolate chips, chopped

 We used a mini ice cream scoop to portion out these fat bombs.

carbs	fibre	fat	protein
1.25g	.2g	20g	1.75g

This recipe needs no introduction. This is fudge at its finest. I promise you will not find a more decadent keto treat than this one. It's melt-in-your-mouth, deliciously delicious fat-tastic fudge.

CHOCOLATE FUDGE TRUFFLES

SERVINGS 12   **SERVING SIZE** 1 truffle

FOR THE TRUFFLE

2	tbsp butter
¼	cup whipping cream (35%)
4	oz cream cheese
¼	cup Swerve or equivalent sweetener (or to taste)
2	tbsp cocoa
1	tsp vanilla
⅛	tsp salt

FOR THE COATING

3	tbsp cocoa
2	tsp Swerve

1. Melt butter in a small saucepan over medium heat.

2. Add whipping cream and cream cheese. Whisk until smooth.

3. Add sweetener and stir constantly, adjust to taste.

4. Turn off heat and stir in cocoa, vanilla, and salt. Blend well.

5. Chill for 3-4 hours in the fridge.

6. Meanwhile, combine the coating ingredients and set aside.

7. Remove truffles from the fridge and roll the batter into balls.

8. Roll the balls in cocoa powder mixture and return to the fridge.

9. Keep refrigerated.

carbs	fibre	fat	protein
2g	.67g	6g	1g

When I think back to favourite childhood treats, Cherry Blossom was right at the top of the list. I don't get to eat Cherry Blossoms these days. I'm sure I'd be mortified at the amount of sugar in one bite, let alone the whole thing. That doesn't mean I have to forgo the whole cherry chocolate experience, though. I've found a way to have my cherries and chocolate and enjoy my slim waistline too!

KETO CHERRY BLOSSOMS

SERVINGS 12   **SERVING SIZE** 1 treat

FOR THE FILLING

1. Cover frozen cherries with water and set aside for one hour.
2. Remove cherries from the water and set both aside.
3. Place cherry water in a small saucepan over medium-low heat.
4. Add Swerve and xanthan gum and whisk until combined.
5. Set aside to thicken.

FOR THE CHOCOLATE

1. Combine all ingredients in a small saucepan.
2. Melt over medium-low heat or in a double boiler.
3. Set aside to cool for 5 minutes.

PUTTING IT ALL TOGETHER

1. Spoon chocolate into silicon moulds. We use a mini ice cube tray with a silicon bottom for easy removal, but any mould with small-sized holes will do. Fill to the top.
2. Place mould into freezer for 5 minutes.
3. Remove moulds and scoop out the inner core of the chocolates.
4. Place a piece or two of cherry in the chocolate core and fill with cherry sauce.
5. Place in the freezer for 5 minutes.
6. Cover the cherry-filled chocolate with the remaining (warmed) chocolate to cover over the hole.
7. Place in the freezer to cool.
8. Store in the fridge.

FOR THE FILLING

12   frozen cherries, chopped into quarters

cherry water (water retained from soaking cherries)

1   tbsp confectioner's Swerve

¼   tsp xanthan gum

FOR THE CHOCOLATE

4   oz unsweetened baking chocolate

¼   cup coconut oil

¼   cup confectioner's Swerve

1   tsp vanilla

⅛   tsp Himalayan pink salt

Finely shredded unsweetened coconut and chopped walnuts can be added to the chocolate mixture. Adjust macros accordingly.

carbs	fibre	fat	protein
3.5g	1.6g	9.5g	1.4g

Key Lime Pie Bites are the perfect combination of zesty lime flavour, creamy goodness, and the silky taste of macadamia nuts all in one little ball.

Regular limes can be substituted for the miniature key limes. The taste will be slightly different, but they will be just as delicious.

Use these Key Lime Pie Bites as a blast of healthy fats or a petite sweet treat at the end of the day.

KEY LIME PIE BITES

SERVINGS 16   **SERVING SIZE** 1 bite

FOR THE CRUST COATING

¼   cup macadamia nuts, blended in a Bullet

2   tbsp Swerve

1   tsp lime zest

Himalayan pink salt to taste

FOR THE KEY LIME PIE

¼   cup confectioner's Swerve

12   oz cream cheese

½   cup macadamia nuts, powdered/grated

⅓   cup coconut oil, melted

3   tbsp lime juice

1   tbsp coconut flour

1   tsp lime zest

1   tsp vanilla extract

1. Combine all crust ingredients and set aside.

2. Cream together Swerve and cream cheese until thoroughly combined.

3. Stir in all remaining ingredients and combine well. Cover and refrigerate until cream cheese mixture has chilled and firmed up slightly.

4. Remove batter from the fridge and roll into balls. (We use a mini ice cream scoop.)

5. Roll the balls in the crust coating.

carbs	fibre	fat	protein
2g	1g	12g	1g

If you love Grandma's/Mom's lemon meringue pie, you're just gonna love this fat bomb recipe. It has all the flavour with nowhere near the amount of carbs. The base of this tart is a delicious crumb biscuit. It adds another flavour and texture dimension to the Lemon Curd (page 231) and meringue.

We hope you enjoy it!

LEMON MERINGUE TARTS

SERVINGS 12   **SERVING SIZE** 1 tart

FOR THE CRUMB BASE

1. Combine all ingredients and press into mini muffin pan.

2. Bake at 350°F for 10 minutes or until crust is light brown.

3. Set aside.

PUTTING IT ALL TOGETHER

1. When crust and Lemon Curd are cooled, spoon curd over crust.

2. Start the meringue by beating egg whites and cream of tartar with a hand mixer in a glass or metal bowl, starting off on low setting, then increasing to medium when the egg whites are foamy. Continue to beat on medium setting until soft peaks form.

3. Slowly add sweetener and vanilla while beating.

4. Continue to beat until stiff peaks form.

5. Spoon meringue onto the top of the tart and swirl.

6. Bake at 350°F for 5-10 minutes or until tops are golden brown.

7. Cool on rack, then refrigerate.

FOR THE CRUMB BASE

1   cup almond flour

¼-½   cup butter, melted

¼   cup confectioner's Swerve

¼   cup flax meal

¼   cup unsweetened shredded coconut

zest of 1 lemon

FOR THE FILLING

Lemon Curd (page 231)

FOR THE MERINGUE

4   large eggs, whites only, room temperature

¼   tsp cream of tartar

¼   cup confectioner's Swerve, or equivalent

½   tsp vanilla extract

 Egg whites must be at room temperature for a successful meringue.

carbs	fibre	fat	protein
3.25g	1.8g	14g	4g

Our Partridgeberry Lemon Fat Bombs are modelled after a loaf my grandmother made years ago. The tart berries and sour lemon flavouring go hand in hand and create a *ba-BAM* of flavour in your mouth and liven up the healthy fats for your body.

The partridgeberries can be swapped out for cranberries or blueberries, but the small red berries native to the East Coast fit the recipe best of all.

PARTRIDGEBERRY LEMON FAT BOMBS

SERVINGS 12   **SERVING SIZE** 1 bomb

2	tbsp butter
¼	cup whipping cream (35%)
4	oz cream cheese
¼	cup Swerve or other sweetener (or to taste)
1	tsp vanilla
⅛	tsp salt
2-3	drops food grade lemon oil (We use LorAnn super concentrated oils.)
24	partridgeberries, chopped finely

1. Melt butter in a small saucepan over medium heat.
2. Add whipping cream and cream cheese. Whisk until smooth.
3. Add sweetener and stir constantly, adjusting to taste.
4. Turn off heat and stir in vanilla, salt, and lemon oil. Blend well.
5. Gently mix in the partridgeberries.
6. Pour into a silicon mini muffin mould lined with paper liners.
7. Chill for 3-4 hours in the freezer.
8. Keep refrigerated.

carbs	fibre	fat	protein
1.4g	.8g	5.3g	.75g

Pumpkin Pie Fat Bombs can be best described as the taste of fall. The combined aroma of cinnamon, ginger, and allspice is as much a part of autumn as are boots, sweaters, and falling leaves.

These Pumpkin Pie Fat Bombs will give you an extra boost of healthy fats and a big hit of yummy in each creamy mouthful. This recipe was built to satisfy my own fall cravings, but the flavour profile may not be strong enough (or too strong) for your tastes. Feel free to tweak the amounts of spices to appease your own taste buds.

PUMPKIN PIE FAT BOMBS

SERVINGS 24   **SERVING SIZE** 2 bombs

1. Combine all ingredients in a medium bowl and beat with a hand mixer until smooth and creamy.

2. Place bowl in the fridge for 30 minutes.

3. Scoop dollops onto a parchment-lined pan or directly into mini cupcake liners.

4. Store in the refrigerator for maximum flavour and texture.

8   oz cream cheese

1   cup pumpkin purée

⅓   cup confectioner's Swerve

½   tbsp cinnamon

1   tsp vanilla

½   tsp ginger

⅛   tsp allspice

⅛   tsp nutmeg

pinch Himalayan pink salt

carbs	fibre	fat	protein
2.25g	.9g	6g	1.6g

Berries are used in moderation in the keto way of eating. As you progress through your own keto journey, you will find that when it comes to sweetness, a little goes a long way. The little beads of raspberry in these vanilla fat bombs act as mini explosions of added flavour and sweetness.

This vanilla base can be used for a multitude of fat bombs. The possibilities are only limited by your keto imagination.

RASPBERRY VANILLA CHEESECAKE BOMBS

SERVINGS 12 **SERVING SIZE** 1 bomb

2	tbsp butter
¼	cup whipping cream (35%)
4	oz cream cheese
3	tsp confectioner's Swerve or equivalent (or to taste)
1	tsp vanilla
⅛	tsp salt
6	raspberries, chopped finely

1. Melt butter in a small saucepan over medium heat.
2. Add whipping cream and cream cheese. Whisk until smooth.
3. Add Swerve and stir, adjusting sweetness to taste.
4. Turn off heat and stir in vanilla and salt. Blend well.
5. Pour into paper liners in a silicon mini muffin mould.
6. Divide raspberry pieces into sections and add them to each fat bomb.
7. Gently mix the raspberries into the batter, trying not to mash the berries or disturb the juices. (We use the handle of a spoon.)
8. Chill for 3-4 hours.
9. Keep refrigerated.

carbs	fibre	fat	protein
.5g	0g	6.7g	.8g

DESSERTS

Cardamom, usually found in Indian cooking, is a unique, pungent taste that we're used to eating in savoury dishes, but sometimes flavours are delightfully surprising when you use them in different ways.

My first sweet application of cardamom was in a quaint Indian café in London. The cardamom tea stood out on the menu and I just had to try it. The tea had bitter and smoky undertones, but overall I tasted the aromatic cardamom paired with cinnamon that was enhanced by the creamy texture of the tea. I knew right then that I had to dig in and invent something sweet for our keto kitchen.

Cardamom Spice Cake is the result of the spark that was lit that day. I thought this spice blend would take many attempts and much practice to make perfect, but the whole family thought this spice cake was absolutely delicious right from the start.

CARDAMOM SPICE CAKE

SERVINGS 12   **SERVING SIZE** 1 slice

2	cups almond flour
¼	cup coconut flour
1	tbsp baking soda
2¼	tsp ground cardamom
1	tsp cream of tartar
1	tsp ground cinnamon
1	tsp ginger
½	tsp salt
1	cup Swerve
½	cup butter
½	cup whipping cream (35%)
½	cup cream cheese
1	tsp vanilla extract
4	large eggs
1	drop orange food grade essential oil (We use LorAnn.)
1	tsp grated lemon zest

1. Preheat oven to 325°F.

2. Grease a Bundt pan with butter. Set aside.

3. Combine dry ingredients (except Swerve) and sift together. Set aside.

4. In another bowl (I use the stand mixer), combine Swerve, butter, whipping cream, and cream cheese. Cream together.

5. Alternate between adding dry mixture, vanilla, and eggs while you mix in between each addition.

6. Add remaining ingredients and mix for 5 minutes on high.

7. Spoon batter into pan. Use your spatula to create a higher amount of batter in the centre of the pan. (The almond flour doesn't rise the same way as wheat flour, so we move the batter to try to create the shape of a risen loaf.)

8. Bake for 55 minutes or until a wooden toothpick inserted in the centre comes out clean.

9. Cool for 5 minutes, then remove from pan.

carbs	fibre	fat	protein
9.5g	4.5g	25g	7g

Years ago, I worked at a shopping mall as a store manager. The manager had to step up and do what needed to be done, and that often meant twelve-hour days and missing out on regular coffee and lunch breaks. The one indulgence I allowed myself every now and then during a slow period when I had a full staff on hand was to sneak away to the quiet little coffee shop for a few moments alone and my special treat: a coffee and a single decadent carrot cake covered with cream cheese frosting.

One little bite of this Carrot Cake takes me right back there. That moment of calm indulgence, just for me. Absolute perfection in one bite. I hope it takes you somewhere special too!

CARROT CAKE

SERVINGS 12   **SERVING SIZE** 1 slice

FOR THE CAKE

1. Combine wet ingredients including coconut, carrot, and walnuts in a large bowl or food processor.

2. Combine all dry ingredients and mix thoroughly to break up any small chunks.

3. Combine dry ingredients into wet, adding the dry a bit at a time.

4. Pour batter into Bundt pan or 10-inch round pan.

5. Bake at 400°F for 10 minutes. Then decrease temp to 350°F and bake for 40-50 more minutes, depending on your oven and chosen pan. Cake is done when toothpick inserted in the middle comes out clean.

6. Set aside to cool.

FOR THE CAKE

1. Whip cream cheese until it's smooth.

2. Add softened butter, whipping cream, Swerve, and vanilla, and whip again until totally combined.

3. Turn the mixer up to high for the last 5 minutes to help the frosting fluff.

 This frosting performs best when it's at room temperature. Refrigerating it before frosting the cake will make it more firm, and as a result it might tear the cake.

FOR THE CAKE

6	large eggs
¾	cup coconut milk or 35% whipping cream
¼	cup extra virgin olive oil
¾	cup shredded coconut
¾	cup carrot, shredded
¼	cup walnuts, chopped (optional)
1	tsp vanilla
1	cup almond flour
½	cup coconut flour
½	cup Swerve
1	tbsp psyllium husk powder
2	tsp ground cinnamon
1	tsp cream of tartar
1	tsp ground ginger
½	tsp baking soda
½	tsp cardamom
½	tsp salt
¼	tsp nutmeg

FOR THE FROSTING

12	oz regular cream cheese, softened
¼	cup butter, softened
¼	cup whipping cream (35%)
½	cup confectioner's Swerve
1	tsp vanilla

carbs	fibre	fat	protein
9.4g	4.5g	26g	7g

FOR THE PECAN CRUST

1½ cups crushed pecans

1   cup flax meal

6   oz butter

⅓   cup confectioner's Swerve

FOR THE CHEESECAKE

4   (8 oz) packages of cream cheese

¾   cup confectioner's Swerve, or to taste

1   tsp vanilla

3   eggs

FOR THE CHOCOLATE SAUCE

4   tbsp butter

3   oz unsweetened baking chocolate

⅓   cup whipping cream (35%)

¼   cup confectioner's Swerve

FOR THE CARAMEL SAUCE

6   tbsp butter

1   cup Swerve

½   cup whipping cream (35%)

½   tsp caramel flavouring (optional)

pecans, for garnish

carbs	fibre	fat	protein
9.75g	5g	70g	11g

When Sidekick Geoff and I first became a we, he swore he didn't like caramel. At the time I smiled and nodded and said not a word. I figured to myself that somewhere deep down in the man I loved there was a small part of him that just HAD to love caramel.

The first time I made this cheesecake for him, he had his with chocolate sauce. I pretended I couldn't finish my own caramel-covered portion and I passed the leftovers over to him. He was hit with a combination of flavours that made his palate dance. His eyes popped out, and he looked at me absolutely agog at what he was experiencing. Yes, ladies and gentlemen, he LOVED the caramel!

CHOCOLATE, CARAMEL AND PECAN CHEESECAKE

SERVINGS 12   **SERVING SIZE** 1 piece

FOR THE CRUST

1.   Mix all ingredients well and press into a greased (or parchment-lined) springform pan. (We use a 9-inch pan.)

2.   Bake at 350°F for 10-12 minutes or until the crust begins to brown slightly. Set aside and let cool.

3.   Turn oven down to 325°F.

FOR THE CHEESECAKE

1.   Place a pan of water in the oven alongside where you will put your cheesecake, or cover the bottom of your cheesecake pan with tinfoil and place it in a deeper pan filled with water for a water bath. This will keep your cheesecake from splitting.

2.   Mix cream cheese, sweetener, and vanilla with a food processor or blender.

3.   Add eggs one at a time, mixing well before adding the next.

4.   Spoon the batter over the crust. Remember that the springform pan is in two pieces and liquid butter will seep out, so make sure you put another pan underneath to catch the drippings.

5.   Bake for 1 hour and 5-10 minutes or until centre is mostly set. There should be the slightest jiggle in the centre when it's done.

6.   Run a knife around the rim of the pan to loosen the cake. Allow it to cool before removing the springform pan ring.

Alternate sweeteners may be used but may not ensure you have proper bulking or consistency.

7. The cake can be eaten when cool but is best when refrigerated overnight.

FOR THE CHOCOLATE SAUCE

1. Melt the butter and chocolate in a saucepan over low heat. Stir constantly and be careful as the chocolate can burn quickly.

2. Add cream and sweetener and stir until smooth and thick.

3. Let cool and pour into a squeeze bottle or a measuring cup with a spout for pouring.

FOR THE CARAMEL SAUCE

1. Heat butter in a saucepan over medium heat until it comes to a rolling boil. Watch very carefully for the butter to darken and for tiny specks of brown to appear.

2. Quickly add sweetener and cream to the browning butter. Whisk until the sauce comes together and becomes smooth.

3. Add caramel flavouring.

4. Let cool and pour into a squeeze bottle or a measuring cup with a spout for pouring.

5. Drizzle both sauces over the individual slices of cheesecake as you serve them. Garnish with pecans placed in piles of three.

We usually do the sauces as a team, with each of us tackling a sauce so they're ready at the same time. You also need to make sure you have all the ingredients at the ready, as both sauces can scorch very quickly.

This may be called Cinnamon Pecan Coffee Cake, but this cake doesn't have to be eaten with a coffee. It goes well with a cup of tea, a glass of almond milk, or even a glass of water.

The base of the Cinnamon Pecan Coffee Cake is multitalented. Remove the cinnamon filling and stir in some blueberries or partridgeberries, or just have the cake plain. It's delicious any ole way.

The batter of this cake is a little heavier than a traditional coffee cake, so we lend a hand by moulding the batter in the pan before it goes into the oven. The batter should be lower by the edges of the pan, but a bit higher toward the centre of the loaf. Take caution not to disturb the cinnamon filling as you're moulding the top.

Walnuts can be substituted for pecans.

Top with our Cream Cheese Frosting (page 212). For added decadence top the frosting with a drizzle of Caramel Sauce (page 288-289).

CINNAMON PECAN COFFEE CAKE

SERVINGS 12   **SERVING SIZE** 1 slice

1. For the base, mix all dry ingredients except Swerve together in a medium bowl. Set aside.

2. Combine filling ingredients and set aside.

3. Cream butter and Swerve together in a stand mixer or a medium bowl with a hand mixer.

4. Add eggs one at a time. Alternate with dry ingredients and crème fraîche/whipping cream, blending between each one.

5. Add vanilla and combine one last time.

6. Pour half the batter into a Bundt pan, making sure you swirl the batter slightly up the sides to create a bit of a V.

7. Spoon two-thirds of the filling mixture over the batter, then top with remaining half of the batter.

8. Tap the cake a couple of times on the counter to help remove any air bubbles.

9. Heap the batter toward the centre of the pan to create the raised portion of the loaf that most people are accustomed to.

10. When you're satisfied with the shape of the cake, sprinkle the remaining cinnamon filling over the top.

11. Bake at 350°F for 1 hour or until toothpick inserted into the centre comes out clean.

12. Let set for 5 minutes before removing from the pan.

FOR THE BASE

2 cups almond flour

¼ cup coconut flour

1½ tsp baking soda

1 tsp cream of tartar

½ tsp salt

1 cup confectioner's Swerve

¾ cup butter, softened

4 large eggs

1 cup crème fraîche (or sour cream)

¼ cup whipping cream (35%)

2 tsp vanilla extract

FOR THE FILLING

½ cup chopped pecans

¼ cup Swerve

1½ tsp ground cinnamon

carbs	fibre	fat	protein
10g	5g	28g	8g

Everybody loves decadent brownies, right? I mean, what's not to love about chocolatey, fudgy brownies? These brownies are super rich, more of a dense fudge type bite. To maximize the unique texture of these decadent treats we recommend you store them in the fridge where the ingredients will firm up.

Our favourite way to eat these Decadent Brownies is as mini cupcakes, or you can bake them in an 8 x 8 pan like a traditional brownie. Top them with our chocolate Cream Cheese Frosting (page 216) and you'll swear you just found yourself a piece of chocolate heaven!

DECADENT BROWNIES

SERVINGS 16   **SERVING SIZE** 1 brownie

½	cup almond flour
½	cup coconut flour
½	cup Swerve or sweetener, to taste
2	tbsp cocoa, heaping
1	tsp baking soda
1	tsp cream of tartar
⅛	tsp Himalayan pink salt
½	cup butter
¼	cup unsweetened baking chocolate
¾	cup whipping cream (35%)
¼	cup cream cheese
3	eggs

1. Combine all dry ingredients and set aside.

2. Melt butter and baking chocolate in microwave or double boiler. Remove from heat and pour into a mixing bowl.

3. Add whipping cream, cream cheese, and eggs into chocolate and combine.

4. Slowly fold dry ingredients into wet mixture and pour into greased baking dish or lined cupcake pan.

5. Bake at 350°F for 15-25 minutes (using the lower end of this range if you're doing mini cupcakes) or until the centre is just set and an inserted toothpick comes out slightly moist.

carbs 5g	fibre 3g	fat 13g	protein 3.3g

 Do not overbake the brownies. Slightly undercook them for a dense, chocolatey bite.

One taste of Gooseberry Ice Cream and I'm transported back to Nan's kitchen. It seemed a magical thing at the time, how Nan gathered up berries in her apron. If you weren't looking carefully, you wouldn't have even noticed she did it. She would combine those berries with some cream and other ingredients from her pantry. Pure magic.

Nan's pantry was nothing like we have today—big barrels of flour and sugar—and the rest came mostly from what she grew. Nan magically transformed those meagre ingredients into the most amazing treats, but none was as special as the gooseberry ice cream. There was a sweetness, but there was also a sour tartness from the berries that made your cheeks tingle.

Gooseberries are hard to come by today unless you're lucky enough to have a plant in your garden. For those of you that do, gather a few in your apron next summer and think of me.

GOOSEBERRY ICE CREAM

SERVINGS 4   **SERVING SIZE** ⅔ cup

1. Blend pureed gooseberries (1) and Swerve in a Bullet. Set aside.

2. In a medium saucepan, combine cream, egg yolks, and salt with a whisk.

3. Using low-medium heat, slowly bring cream mixture to a point where it's starting to steam, whisking constantly. As soon as it starts to steam, remove from heat.

4. Whisk in berry mix as well as chopped berries (2).

5. Move all ingredients to a blender or Bullet and blend for 2 minutes on high.

6. Transfer to a container and place in the freezer for a minimum of 1 hour and a maximum of 3 days.

⅔ cup gooseberries, pureed (1)

½ confectioner's Swerve

2 cups whipping cream (35%)

4 large egg yolks

⅛ tsp Himalayan pink salt

1 tsp vanilla

½ cup gooseberries, chopped (2)

Ice cream with sweeteners will not freeze the same as regular ice cream. Remove from the freezer a half-hour in advance to allow it to soften.

Gooseberries can be substituted for any other berry.

carbs	fibre	fat	protein
8g	2g	47.5g	9g

The icing can be spread on these donuts as is, but my favourite way is to slightly warm the icing in a small saucepan and dip the donuts in for that smooth glazed look.

Recipe can also be used for individual muffins or cupcakes.

This is a recipe that has been passed down in my family. I remember my grandmother's handwritten version, scrawled on a piece of loose-leaf and tucked into her favourite recipe book for safekeeping.

Back in the day, they didn't have the concentrated food grade essential oils—they used the zest and juice of lemons to get that flavour. This recipe uses a combination of the way Nan used to do it and my own ketofied version. You can buy the essential oil at any store where good quality baking ingredients are sold. If you're using it, make sure to use only a drop—this stuff is super concentrated. I use an ⅛ teaspoon measure to drop the oil in to make sure I don't accidentally add too much to the batter.

LEMON POPPYSEED DONUT

SERVINGS 8   **SERVING SIZE** 1 donut

FOR THE DONUTS

1	cup almond flour
½	cup coconut flour
⅓	cup confectioner's Swerve
½	tsp cream of tartar
¼	tsp baking soda
2	eggs
⅔	cup sour cream
⅓	cup whipping cream (35%)
1	tsp of vanilla extract
1	lemon, zest and juice
1	drop lemon essential oil
1	tbsp poppy seeds

FOR THE FROSTING

4	oz cream cheese, softened
½	cup confectioner's Swerve
2	tbsp whipping cream (35%)
2	tbsp butter
1	tbsp lemon juice
⅛	drop lemon oil

FOR THE DONUTS

1. Preheat oven to 350°F.
2. Combine all dry ingredients, with the exception of poppyseeds, in a large mixing bowl and set aside. (We use a whisk to make sure the lumps are broken up.)
3. Combine wet ingredients in a medium-sized bowl and mix well with a hand mixer or whisk.
4. Create a well in the centre of the dry ingredients and pour the wet ingredients into the well.
5. Slowly incorporate the wet mixture into the dry ingredients with a hand mixer or whisk.
6. When both are combined, use a spatula to fold in the poppy-seeds.
7. Spoon the mixture into a donut pan. Fill each section three-quarters full.
8. Bake for 20-25 minutes, or until a toothpick comes out clean when inserted in the donut.
9. Cool donuts in the pan.

FOR THE FROSTING

1. Thoroughly cream ingredients together with a mixer. Use immediately.

carbs	fibre	fat	protein
10g	4g	29g	8g

I've always been a chocoholic, and this milk chocolate recipe allows me to continue with my indulgent pleasure and still stay in ketosis.

This is an adaptation of our Pecan and Macadamia Chocolate Bark recipe (see page 307) for those of us who enjoy a creamier, richer, sweet chocolate treat.

MILK CHOCOLATE

SERVINGS 16   **SERVING SIZE** 1 large piece

1. Chop chocolate into small pieces or slivers and set aside.

2. Heat coconut oil, cream, and crème fraîche in a double boiler or microwave, being careful not to burn.

3. Stir in Swerve and remove from heat.

4. Stir in chocolate pieces and vanilla and mix well with a whisk.

5. Cool slightly. (We wait for 1 minute.)

6. Pour/spoon chocolate mix over baking sheet lined with parchment paper.

7. Sprinkle Himalayan pink salt over the top of the bark (to taste) and chill for 2 hours.

8. Break chocolate into pieces and store in a sealed container in the fridge.

4	oz unsweetened baking chocolate
2	tbsp solid coconut oil or butter
4	oz whipping cream (35%)
4	oz crème fraîche or sour cream
¼	cup confectioner's Swerve
1	tsp vanilla
⅛	tsp Himalayan pink salt

 For an added kick, sprinkle chili powder over the top of the chocolate before cooling.

carbs	fibre	fat	protein
2g	1.3g	16g	1.5g

It just wouldn't be a Newfoundland cookbook without a recipe for Newfoundland Snowballs. Snowballs are a cookie that is a constant in Newfoundland households at Christmastime and also a go-to for many plates of weekend sweets.

The coconut and chocolate flavours that you've grown to love are given a bit of a boost with some crème fraîche or cream cheese. The crème fraîche will give you a lighter consistency, while the cream cheese will make the Newfoundland Snowballs a little more fudgy and decadent. We replaced the oatmeal with a combination of almond flour and flax meal for a healthier and keto-friendly version of yummy.

We think these Newfoundland Snowballs are even better than the non-keto equivalent.

FOR THE COATING

- 1   cup shredded unsweetened coconut
- 2   tbsp confectioner's Swerve

FOR THE COOKIE

- 1½   cup almond flour
- 1   cup crème fraîche or cream cheese
- 1   cup flax meal
- 1   cup unsweetened fine coconut
- ¾   cup butter
- ¾   cup Swerve or equivalent
- 2   tbsp cocoa
- 1   tbsp psyllium husk
- 1   tsp vanilla
- pinch salt

NEWFOUNDLAND SNOWBALLS

SERVINGS 24   **SERVING SIZE** 1 snowball

1. Mix coating ingredients. Set aside.

2. Place all cookie ingredients in a medium saucepan and simmer over low heat, stirring constantly.

3. When batter has totally come together and ingredients are melted, transfer pot to fridge to cool for 30 minutes.

4. Use a scoop or your hands to form the batter into small balls.

5. Roll balls in coating.

6. Store in the fridge.

carbs	fibre	fat	protein
5g	3g	20g	3g

If you're not from Newfoundland or near vicinity, I wouldn't expect you to know that No Bake Bakeapple Cheesecake uses no apples.

Bakeapples (a.k.a. cloudberries) are a Newfoundland and Labrador delicacy. They grow close to the ground in bogs and marshes and are part of the raspberry family; they look like a peach-coloured or orange raspberry. They have a unique tart and tangy taste that does well in cakes, cookies, and ice creams, but they are most often just spooned out of the jar.

In this no bake cheesecake, the base is baked, but the cream cheese filling is not.

NO BAKE BAKEAPPLE CHEESECAKE

SERVINGS 12   **SERVING SIZE** 1 slice

FOR THE BASE

1. Combine all ingredients and press into 9-inch springform pan.

2. Bake at 300°F for 10 minutes with a piece of tinfoil over the top so the crust doesn't burn.

3. Remove the tinfoil, turn off the oven, and put the crust back in the oven for 5 minutes.

4. Remove from the oven and set aside to cool.

FOR THE CHEESECAKE

1. Combine all filling ingredients in a medium bowl.

2. Beat on high setting of your hand mixer for about 5 minutes, or until all items are creamy and there are no lumps.

3. Spoon onto the crust and level the filling with a spatula.

4. Combine berries and Swerve and mash slightly.

5. Spoon berry topping over the cream cheese filling.

6. Refrigerate for at least 2 hours before serving.

FOR THE BASE

1½ cups almond flour

¼   cup butter, melted

2   tbsp confectioner's Swerve

pinch Himalayan pink salt

FOR THE FILLING

2   (8 oz) packages cream cheese

1   cup crème fraîche or sour cream

½   cup confectioner's Swerve

2   tsp vanilla

pinch Himalayan pink salt

FOR THE TOPPING

2   cups bakeapples (any type of berries can be substituted)

⅓   cup confectioner's Swerve

carbs	fibre	fat	protein
5g	1.5g	31g	6g

Any Newfoundlander who has driven through the centre of St. John's is familiar with the heavenly smell of Jam Jams wafting from inside Purity Factories. When my son Alex was little, no matter where we were in town or what we had to do, he would ask to drive by the cookie place, just so he could "sniff the cookies." Let me tell you, we had many drive-by sniffings.

Our keto version of Jam Jams uses almond and coconut flours and Swerve to sweeten the dough. We recommend a partridgeberry filling, but the more traditional raspberry is always an option.

I still can't drive past that neighbourhood without thinking of that little guy in the backseat of my car and how much he loved to go by there. We hope this recipe makes your kitchen smell like your very own version of heaven. Just don't forget to take the time to sniff those cookies.

FOR THE COOKIE

1	cup butter
¾	cup Swerve
1	egg
1¼	tsp baking soda, dissolved in 3 tbsp hot water
1	tsp vanilla
1	cup almond flour
¼	cup coconut flour
1	tsp cream of tartar
½	tsp salt

FOR THE FILLING

Partridgeberry Sauce (page 236)

OLD-FASHIONED JAM JAMS

SERVINGS 12   **SERVING SIZE** 1 Jam Jam

1. Cream together butter, Swerve, egg, water/baking soda, and vanilla.

2. In a separate bowl, combine cream of tartar, salt, and flours.

3. Combine dry and wet ingredients.

4. Form dough into 24 balls and place them on a cookie sheet, allowing space for the cookies to spread.

5. Bake at 350°F for 8-10 minutes.

6. Cool completely.

7. When cool, spread Partridgeberry Sauce atop one cookie, then top with another to form a cookie sandwich with the sauce in the middle.

carbs	fibre	fat	protein
6g	3.4g	21g	4g

Chocolate. It seems to be that one thing that many of us can't do without. I can tell you that personally, I've checked the labels of dozens and dozens of different diet-type chocolate bars, only to be mortified at either the carb count or the ugly ingredients. I (we) even broke down and brought some home. Of those, some were sent home with other family members and, I confess, a small amount was consumed here.

Eventually, my sensible side kicked in. What's the sense of eating all this healthy food and then throwing it all down the tube for one piece of chocolate? It just doesn't make sense. So, that's how and why our version of keto chocolate bark was born. In this recipe we use macadamia nuts and pecans, but you can substitute any type of nuts (or other ingredients that you prefer). Just remember to keep the carb counts (and ingredients list) in mind for any items that you switch out.

PECAN AND MACADAMIA CHOCOLATE BARK

SERVINGS 12   **SERVING SIZE** 1 piece

1. Chop nuts into small pieces. Scatter pieces on a parchment-covered baking sheet.

2. Melt chocolate and coconut oil in a double boiler or microwave, being careful not to burn.

3. Stir in Swerve and vanilla and remove from heat. Cool slightly (we wait for 1 minute).

4. Pour/spoon chocolate mix over scattered nuts and chill for 2 hours.

5. Sprinkle Himalayan pink salt over the top of the bark.

6. Break bark into 12 pieces.

3   oz macadamia nuts, chopped

3   oz pecans, chopped

3   oz unsweetened baking chocolate

2   tbsp solid coconut oil

¼   cup confectioner's Swerve (or equivalent), to taste

1   tsp vanilla

⅛   tsp Himalayan pink salt

carbs	fibre	fat	protein
3g	2.25g	17g	2g

Place a separate pan with water in the oven to help keep the cheesecake from splitting.

We put tinfoil on the edge of the cheesecake to keep it from browning too much.

Thanksgiving dinner is just not the same without Nan's perfect pumpkin pie on the table. Her pumpkin pie was a wonder—the spices were always balanced with the perfect amount of sweetness, and the crust was just the right amount of crispy. It was always spot on.

This recipe can be made any time of year, but autumn is when pumpkins come to mind for me. It might be the orangey-red of the leaves as they fall from the trees or the colour of the pumpkins as they ripen. Or maybe it's because everybody is wondering what to do with the insides of their pumpkins after they carve their jack-o'-lanterns.

I hope I did Nan justice by ketofying this recipe. I hope that if she were still here with us, I would have her stamp of approval on this one.

PERFECT PUMPKIN CHEESECAKE

SERVINGS 12   **SERVING SIZE** 1 slice

FOR THE CRUST

2   cups almond flour

½   cup butter

¼   cup Swerve

FOR THE PIE

1   (15 oz) can pumpkin

¾   cup granulated Swerve

1   tsp cinnamon

½   tsp ginger

½   tsp salt

¼   tsp cloves

¼   tsp nutmeg

3   (8 oz) packages cream cheese

1   tsp vanilla

3   large eggs

FOR THE CRUST

1. Combine almond flour, butter, and Swerve in a bowl until thoroughly mixed.

2. Press into a springform pan and bake at 325°F for 15 minutes or until golden brown. Set aside to cool.

FOR THE PIE

1. Combine the pumpkin, Swerve, spices, and salt in a medium saucepan and stir over medium heat until thickened and slightly shiny.

2. Combine cream cheese and pumpkin mixture in a stand mixer and mix until thoroughly combined.

3. Add vanilla and then eggs one at a time, mixing between each one.

4. Pour batter on top of cooked crust and bake at 325°F for 1.5 hours or until there is no jiggle in the centre of the cheesecake.

5. Remove from oven and set aside to cool.

6. Serve with whipped 35% cream.

carbs 10g	fibre 3g	fat 36g	protein 10g

Pineapple Weed Cheesecake is a delightful, rich, New York-style cheesecake that has the lightest pineapple taste. The crispy, chewy vanilla crust marries well with the delicate flavour of the pineapple weed cheesecake topping. Together they create a symphony of flavour that you and yours will love.

Pineapple weed can be replaced with any berry or alternate flavour, but to me there's something magical about a dessert that comes from ingredients that happen to grow in your own backyard. I have walked on this weed my whole life and had no idea it had a mild pineapple scent and flavour, let alone that it was edible.

Pineapple weed can be made into jams, jellies, or tea, but my favourite will always be this Pineapple Weed Cheesecake.

Serve with a dollop of fresh whipped cream.

PINEAPPLE WEED CHEESECAKE

SERVINGS 12   **SERVING SIZE** 1 slice

FOR THE CRUST

1. Combine all ingredients in a bowl until thoroughly mixed.

2. Press into a springform pan and bake at 325°F for 15 minutes or until golden brown. Set aside to cool.

FOR THE FILLING

1. Mix sweetener and pineapple weed in a Bullet or blender.

2. Combine sweetener mix with cream cheese.

3. Add vanilla and eggs, one at a time, mixing well before adding the next.

4. Spoon the batter over the crust. Remember the springform pan is in two pieces and liquid butter will seep out, so make sure you put another pan underneath to catch the drippings.

5. Bake for 1 hour or until centre is mostly set. There should be the slightest jiggle in the centre when it's done.

6. Run a knife around the rim of the pan to loosen the cake and allow it to cool before removing the springform ring.

7. Cake can be eaten when cool but is best when refrigerated overnight.

FOR THE CRUST

1	cup almond flour
½	cup butter, softened
¼	cup Swerve

FOR THE FILLING

¾	cup confectioner's Swerve, to taste
¼-½	cup pineapple weed (or alternate berry)
4	(8 oz) packages of cream cheese
1	tsp vanilla
3	eggs

carbs	fibre	fat	protein
4.8g	1g	37g	9g

Rhubarb Sour Cream Cookies will be the lightest and most fluffy cookies that you will ever remember tasting. Rhubarb can be substituted with any berry, but in my opinion rhubarb is a perfect fit for this recipe.

Many old-time Newfoundland and Labrador gardens had a corner with rhubarb growing. It seems to out of fashion these days, being replaced by fruits from the supermarket. But rhubarb is a great low-carb fruit alternative with loads of fibre to keep you on track.

RHUBARB SOUR CREAM COOKIES

SERVINGS 24   **SERVING SIZE** 1 cookie

1	cup almond flour
½	cup coconut flour
1	tsp baking soda
½	tsp cream of tartar
½	tsp salt
¾	cup Swerve
½	cup butter, softened
1	egg
¾	cup sour cream
½	tsp vanilla extract
1	cup rhubarb, diced

1. Preheat oven to 350°F.

2. In a medium bowl, combine dry ingredients, except Swerve.

3. In a large bowl, cream the butter and Swerve together.

4. Add the egg, sour cream, and vanilla to the butter mix, and mix again until light and fluffy.

5. Slowly add the dry ingredients, using a mixer.

6. Stir in the rhubarb with a spoon or spatula.

7. Drop spoonfuls of batter, about 2 inches apart, onto baking sheets lined with parchment paper.

8. Bake 10-12 minutes or until the edges of the cookies start to brown.

9. Let cool 5 minutes, then move to a rack to cool completely.

carbs	fibre	fat	protein
3g	1.4g	8g	2g

Serve one or two of these cookies on top of a bowl of Vanilla Cheesecake Ice Cream (page 325) for an extra special treat.

Strawberry rhubarb crumble brings me back to my grandmother's house. I was nine years old and I was out in the flower garden with my Nan. Most of the yard was Pop's domain—vegetables planted row by row and a cute little chicken coop up in the back corner. But the flower garden was Nan's. It was full of so many good scents: daffodils, lilies, gladiolas, and roses galore. Way over on one side, hidden from sight from any young fella who might have gotten it in his head to steal the tender fruits during a midnight raid, was the berry garden.

As I walked behind Nan on this particular day, we passed the spicy scent of gooseberries, the tart, almost sour smell of the black currants, and then found the real joy—the rhubarb plants, right next to a small section of wild strawberries. Now, I know most of you have eaten those big strawberries they sell at the supermarket, but nothing was as sweet as those little gems that Nan nurtured along every year. They were so sweet, they almost made the insides of your cheeks hurt. A memory of pure pleasure.

This strawberry rhubarb crumble has been made keto-friendly. It will even trick your own siblings into thinking they're back in Nan's garden.

If crumble turns out drier than you like, melt some butter in the microwave and brush it on top of the compiled dish. It will soak in and add a moist element to the squares.

Instead of reducing the filling you can sprinkle in xanthan gum to thicken it. Add about ¼ teaspoon and let the filling cool. If the filling is not thick enough, sprinkle in more. Continue to do that until you reach the desired consistency. (We use a shaker to sprinkle in xanthan gum so that it's evenly spread and doesn't clump.)

STRAWBERRY RHUBARB CRUMBLE SQUARES

SERVINGS 8   **SERVING SIZE** 1 square

1. Combine ingredients for the filling in a medium saucepan. Simmer over low-medium heat for 10-15 minutes or until fruit has turned to the consistency of a thick sauce. Set aside.

2. Combine crumble ingredients in a bowl until the whole mix is crumbly. Set aside ½ cup of the crumble.

3. Press remaining crumble into a greased 9-inch pan.

4. Pour the fruit mixture over the crust and spread evenly.

5. Sprinkle the remaining ½ cup of crumble over the fruit mixture.

6. Cover with tinfoil and bake for about 20 minutes at 350°F.

7. Remove foil and bake for another 10 minutes, until crumble is browned.

8. Cool and serve.

FOR THE FILLING

1	cup strawberries
1	cup rhubarb
½	cup confectioner's Swerve
2	tbsp lemon juice

FOR THE CRUMBLE

1	cup butter, room temperature
¾	cup shredded coconut
½	cup flax meal
¼	cup coconut flour
¼	cup confectioner's Swerve
¼	cup psyllium husk

carbs	fibre	fat	protein
14g	6.75g	34g	3g

Spruce Tip Ice Cream was, for us, the introduction to foraging in our own backyard. When I was reading through a book on what plants were edible in my home province of Newfoundland, I was surprised to see evergreen trees listed there. Spruce buds were of particular interest to me, as my backyard is full of grand spruce trees. After doing my research, I learned that the new spring growth is tender, full of flavour, and very good to eat. Wait until the papery tip breaks open, and harvest from a familiar area. Only harvest a maximum of one-third of these delicate little buds.

This light, citrus-like ice cream will cool you down and delight your tongue with its unique flavour. Enjoy it with an Old-fashioned Jam Jam (page 304).

SPRUCE TIP ICE CREAM

SERVINGS 4   **SERVING SIZE** ½ cup

¼   cup young spruce buds

½   confectioner's Swerve

2   cup whipping cream (35%)

4   large egg yolks

1   tsp vanilla

⅛   tsp Himalayan pink salt

1. Blend spruce tips and Swerve in a Bullet. Set aside.

2. In a medium saucepan, combine cream, egg yolks, vanilla, and salt with a whisk.

3. Using low-medium heat, slowly bring cream mixture to a point where it's starting to steam, whisking constantly. As soon as it starts to steam, remove from heat.

4. Whisk in spruce tip/Swerve combination.

5. Move all ingredients to a blender or Bullet and blend for 2 minutes on high.

6. Transfer to a container and place in the freezer for a minimum of 1 hour and a maximum of 3 days.

carbs	fibre	fat	protein
5g	1.25g	47g	5g

We try to get many opinions on our recipes as we test them. We all have different likes and dislikes, and we don't just go on our own food preference for our recipes. Spruce Tip Shortbread Cookies challenged the palates of our entire tasting team. Their flavour is unfamiliar to most people. The team all loved it but just couldn't define it. I would say that these cookies have a light, delightful, citrusy flavour that almost tastes like spring.

Harvest your spruce tips (or other evergreen tips) in the springtime when the papery husks start to break open to reveal the soft, vibrant green, new growth. The rule of thumb is not to harvest more than one-third of the tips of any given tree, for sustainability.

These Spruce Tip Shortbread Cookies can be made as just regular old shortbread cookies by omitting the ground spruce tips, but we think they add a fresh layer to the recipe. We vacuum-seal small packets of tips and freeze them for a taste of spring any time of year.

SPRUCE TIP SHORTBREAD COOKIES

SERVINGS 12   **SERVING SIZE** 1 cookie

1	cup almond flour
¼	cup coconut flour
½	cup confectioner's Swerve
¼	cup spruce tips
½	cup butter, softened
⅛	tsp Himalayan pink salt
1	large egg
1	tsp vanilla

1. Preheat oven to 300°F.

2. Combine flours in a small mixing bowl.

3. Combine Swerve and spruce tips in a Bullet and blend for 1 minute.

4. Cream together butter, salt, and spruce tip mixture.

5. Add the egg and vanilla into the butter mixture and mix well.

6. Slowly incorporate dry ingredients into butter mixture.

7. Roll dough into 12 small balls and place them on a cookie sheet.

8. Leave space between the cookies to allow them to spread.

carbs	fibre	fat	protein
3.3g	1.8g	13g	3g

When I was younger, I would always look forward to springtime and a trip to the local Tim Hortons for a strawberry tart. They were only available for a limited time each year, but boy did I make the best of that short window! For me, this recipe brings back childhood, spring, and family time all rolled into one delicious bite.

Our version of the strawberry custard tart has a cookie crumb base which, in our opinion, really adds to the overall dish. We prefer to cook this as a family-style dish, but it can be cooked in individual tarts. This recipe has been a family favourite for years. When we started to ketofy recipes, this one was right at the top of the list!

We hope you enjoy it.

STRAWBERRY CUSTARD TART

SERVINGS 12   **SERVING SIZE** 1 slice

FOR THE BASE

1	cup almond flour
¼-½	cup butter, melted
¼	cup confectioner's Swerve
¼	cup flax meal
¼	cup unsweetened shredded coconut

FOR THE CUSTARD

1	cup cold water
2	tbsp butter
2	oz cream cheese
2	eggs
2	egg yolks (Reserve whites for future use.)
1	cup Swerve
½	tsp xanthan gum

strawberries, cut into ¼-inch slices

FOR THE BASE

1. Combine all ingredients and press into a flan or springform pan.

2. Bake at 350°F for 15-17 minutes or until crust is light brown.

3. Set aside to cool.

FOR THE CUSTARD

1. Combine first 3 ingredients in a medium saucepan.

2. Simmer for 10 minutes.

3. In a separate bowl, whisk eggs and egg yolks.

4. Slowly whisk the hot liquid into the egg (i.e., temper the eggs).

5. Add sweetener.

6. Whisk in xanthan a little bit at a time.

7. Cook over medium heat for 5 minutes, stirring constantly.

8. Set aside to cool.

carbs	fibre	fat	protein
4.3g	2.2g	17g	5g

 Reduce baking time to 7-10 minutes if doing individual tarts.

1. Spoon custard over crust.

2. Arrange strawberries over the top of the custard.

3. Refrigerate for 1 hour before serving

This recipe caused quite a stir when we released it on social media. We had just signed our book contract with Breakwater Books and had decided that some of our recipes should remain as cookbook exclusive, and this was our first exclusive teaser recipe, an excerpt of what you could expect in the pages of our forthcoming book.

What we didn't expect was the onslaught of people asking "OMG, can I have that recipe please?" over and over again.

Out of all the recipes we had to choose from, we knew this one had to make it between the covers. Hope you feel it was worth the wait!

TUXEDO BROWNIES

SERVINGS 16   **SERVING SIZE** 1 brownie

FOR THE BROWNIE LAYER

1 cup almond flour

¼ tsp Himalayan pink salt

4 oz unsweetened baker's chocolate, coarsely chopped

½ cup butter, room temperature

¾ cup confectioner's Swerve

2 large eggs

1 tsp vanilla extract

FOR THE CHEESECAKE

8 oz cream cheese, room temperature

½ cup confectioner's Swerve

1 large egg, room temperature

1 tsp pure vanilla extract

FOR THE GANACHE

4 oz unsweetened baker's chocolate

¼ cup whipping cream

FOR THE BROWNIE LAYER

1. Preheat oven to 350°F.

2. Combine almond flour and salt and set aside.

3. Place chocolate and butter in a double boiler or melt in the microwave.

4. Cream in Swerve.

5. Add eggs, one at a time.

6. Add vanilla.

7. Incorporate dry ingredients into wet batter.

FOR THE CHEESECAKE

1. Combine all ingredients in a medium bowl with a hand or stand mixer.

PUTTING IT ALL TOGETHER

1. Spoon three-quarters of the brownie batter into a 9 x 9 cake pan.

2. Dollop the cheesecake batter on top of the brownie mixture and gently spread it over the other batter, being careful not to disturb the brownie layer.

 Line cake pan with parchment paper for easy removal.

carbs	fibre	fat	protein
6.3g	3.1g	25g	6g

3. Now dollop spoonfuls of the reserved brownie mixture onto the cheesecake layer.

4. Gently swirl the top brownie batter into the cheesecake layer using the tip of a knife for a marble effect.

5. Bake for 20 minutes or until a toothpick inserted into the centre comes out clean.

6. Allow to cool for 10 minutes before removing from pan.

FOR THE GANACHE

1. Melt chocolate in a double boiler or in the microwave, being careful not to let it burn.

2. When the chocolate has totally melted, add the whipping cream and combine with a whisk.

3. Spoon over brownies for a decadent frosting.

 Store brownies in the fridge in an airtight container for up to 5 days.

"I Scream, You Scream, We All Scream for Ice Cream" is a popular song first published in 1927. We often hear "screams" for ice cream recipes on keto forums. To answer your question, Yes! There is a way we can have ice cream.

This is my version of a cream cheese or cheesecake ice cream. It's best eaten within 24 hours. There are no stabilizers in this recipe, so after that timeframe it gets too hard. If you do leave it after the 24-hour mark, just let it sit in the fridge for about 30 minutes or so to soften before serving.

VANILLA CHEESECAKE ICE CREAM

SERVINGS 4   **SERVING SIZE** ⅓ cup

1. Blend all ingredients (except berries, if you are using them) with an immersion blender for 5 minutes.

2. Place in a container and freeze for 3-24 hours.

1   cup whipping cream (35%)

¼   cup cream cheese

2   tbsp Swerve

1   tsp vanilla extract

⅛   tsp Himalayan pink salt

Most of the carbs are in the cream cheese, which can be omitted for a lower carb version.

Add berries for berry ice cream.

Add 2 tablespoons of cocoa for chocolate ice cream.

carbs	fibre	fat	protein
3g	.25g	26g	2g

FLAVOUR PROFILES

The ultimate dish is said to have all the taste components: sweet, bitter, salty, sour, and savoury (also known by the Japanese term *umami*). It takes a talented chef with years of training and/or a passion and natural feel for food to know how to balance these items together in one dish. Spices are an integral part of this equation, and knowing how to use them is key.

Ugly ingredients hide in commercially-prepared spice mixes. For this reason, we recommend you learn to make your own flavour profiles using these basic spice combination recipes. That way there are no nasty surprises.

These spice mixes are based on our own personal tastes. Feel free to fool around with the measurements to find the right level of seasoning for you and your family.

BBQ DRY SPICE/RUB MIX

- 2 tbsp Himalayan pink salt
- 1 tbsp chili powder
- 1 tbsp cumin
- 1 tbsp garlic
- 1 tbsp granulated onion
- 1 tbsp smoked paprika
- 1 tbsp confectioner's Swerve
- ½ tsp black pepper
- ¼ tsp cayenne pepper

CAJUN SPICE MIX

- ¼ cup garlic powder
- 3 tbsp Himalayan pink salt or sea salt
- 3 tbsp smoked paprika
- 2 tbsp onion powder
- 1 tbsp cayenne pepper
- 1 tbsp oregano
- 1 tbsp pepper
- 1 tsp thyme

CHAI SPICE MIX

- 2 tbsp ground ginger
- 3 tsp cinnamon
- 2 tsp allspice
- 2 tsp cardamom
- 2 tsp cloves
- ⅓ tsp black pepper

CHINESE FIVE-SPICE POWDER

- 2 tbsp ground anise
- 1 tbsp ground fennel
- 1 tbsp ground Szechuan peppercorn
- 2 tsp ground cinnamon
- ½ tsp ground cloves

CURRY SPICE MIX

- 2 tbsp coriander
- 2 tbsp cumin
- 1½ tbsp turmeric
- 2 tsp ground ginger
- 1 tsp cinnamon
- 1 tsp dry mustard
- 1 tsp fenugreek
- 1 tsp Himalayan pink salt
- ½ tsp black pepper
- ½ tsp cardamom
- ½ tsp cayenne pepper

GARAM MASALA

- 1 tbsp cardamom
- 2 tsp curry powder
- 1 tsp chili
- 1 tsp pepper
- ½ tsp cinnamon
- ½ tsp cloves
- ⅓ tsp nutmeg

HERBES DE PROVENCE MIX

¼ cup marjoram
2 tbsp rosemary
2 tbsp summer savory
1 tsp fennel
1 tsp lavender
1 tsp orange zest, dried
½ tsp thyme

ITALIAN SPICE MIX

1½ tsp garlic powder
1½ tsp oregano
1 tsp onion powder
1 tsp thyme
½ tsp basil
½ tsp rosemary
½ tsp sage
¼ tsp red pepper flakes

JERK SPICE MIX

2 tbsp garlic powder
1 tbsp allspice
1 tbsp cayenne pepper
4 tsp Himalayan pink salt
4 tsp confectioner's Swerve
1½ tsp dry mustard
1½ tsp onion powder
1½ tsp thyme
1 tsp pepper
1 tsp nutmeg
⅛ tsp cloves

LEMON PEPPER MIX

6 tbsp pepper
6 tbsp Himalayan pink salt
1 tsp lemon zest

MEXICAN SPICE MIX

2 tsp chili powder
2 tsp garlic powder
2 tsp smoked paprika
1½ tsp ground cumin
1 tsp onion powder
½ tsp black pepper
½ tsp crushed red pepper flakes
½ tsp Himalayan pink salt
¼ tsp dried oregano
pinch cinnamon
pinch cloves

PUMPKIN SPICE

3 tbsp cinnamon
1 tsp allspice
1 tsp ginger
½ tsp cloves
½ tsp nutmeg
pinch salt

STEAK SPICE MIX

1 tbsp dehydrated minced onion
1 tbsp garlic powder
1 tbsp pepper
1 tbsp thyme
½ tbsp crushed red pepper flakes
½ tbsp rosemary
1 tsp fennel seed

Blend all ingredients or grind in a mortar and pestle.

TACO SEASONING

⅓ cup chili powder
¼ cup cumin
2 tbsp garlic powder
2 tbsp onion powder
1 tbsp Himalayan pink or sea salt
1 tsp oregano
1 tsp pepper
1 tsp smoked paprika

KETO SWEETENERS
THE GOOD, THE BAD, AND THE UGLY

Nothing strikes fear in a ketonian more than that of spiking insulin in their body. All our research shows that the very basis of ketosis relies on keeping one's insulin levels or Glycemic Index even and stable throughout the day instead of the crazy highs and lows associated with the Western diet.

The very mention of sweeteners and sweet treats in a keto group is enough to create a frenzy of differing opinions, each countering the previous one. The bigger question is, are sweets a good option at all for a ketogenic lifestyle? Studies have shown that the very act of holding a sweet substance in your mouth, without even swallowing, will cause an insulin response.

In my role as administrator for a growing keto community on Facebook, one of the first questions I am often asked by new members concerns what sweeteners are best. My advice is always to hold off and give your body a chance to heal. It's had a lifetime of trying to process chemicals and an abundance of sugar-laden foods. Right now, it just needs a chance to catch up and get used to the new directive you are giving it, to relearn how to rid itself of the toxins that were a part of its everyday life. If you switch from a Western diet and go right into high gear in keto substitutes, you may be doing more harm than good.

When you've been in ketosis for a while and your body has adjusted, then slowly start to add some keto food replacements for sweet treats. Here are some things to keep in mind regarding sweeteners when you feel you're ready to add them into your diet.

1. NATURAL DOESN'T MEAN IT'S KETO!

The blunt reality is that many sweeteners have too many carbs for a ketogenic lifestyle. Take a look at the carb counts of some sweeteners in comparison to ordinary table sugar, which has 4.2 grams of carbohydrates per teaspoon; each of these has at least as many. They may be natural, but they are far from keto.

- brown sugar: 4.5 grams
- maple syrup: 4.5 grams
- turbinado sugar: 4.6 grams
- molasses: 5 grams
- agave nectar: 5.3 grams
- honey: 5.75 grams

2. CHECK FOR FILLERS

You only need a tiny amount of most sweeteners to get the same sweetness as a tablespoon of sugar. Consequently, most companies add fillers to sweeteners so they can be measured like sugar.

That's bad news for most people. Additives such as maltodextrin and dextrose are sugars in disguise. These ingredients are doing you no favours, especially for people who are living with diabetes. The amount of fillers in these ingredients won't break the carb bank, but they can certainly spike insulin and are best avoided. In general, liquid formula sweeteners tend to be safer in this regard, but we still recommend you check ingredients, each and every time.

3. USING SWEETENERS CAN INCREASE CRAVINGS AND STALL WEIGHT LOSS

Scientific studies show that using any sweeteners, even those that have a Glycemic Index of zero and zero calories, might make it harder to lose weight. By adding sweeteners you will significantly increase the reward sensation that you get with sugary foods. This sweet reward sensation can bounce off the pleasure receptors in your brain and trigger cravings. This in turn can significantly increase not only the risk that you'll eat more than you need, but also the possibility that it might derail your dietary way of eating. This can stall you, slow down weight loss, or even cause weight gain.

Studies also show that even adding non-caloric sweeteners to diet beverages may make it harder to lose weight. If you're someone who has difficulty with this, you might be better off just avoiding sweeteners altogether. For most people, sugary cravings decrease over time, which will make it easier to avoid sweeteners as you journey on your keto path.

4. TAKE CARE OF YOUR GUT

Remember to look at the bigger picture of your overall health. Some sweeteners such as xylitol, malitol, or erythritol are known to disrupt the gut microbiome in certain people, leading to digestive distress such as gas and bloating.

More and more research is pointing to gut health as an indicator of potential metabolic issues. We all have a mixture of good and bad bacteria, but sometimes the bad guys get the upper hand. This imbalance has the potential to make you sick and can play a role in a number of health conditions.

While we still have much to learn about managing a healthy gut, we all—particularly those who are dealing with insulin resistance or blood sugar issues—need to take steps to maintain the right balance for our own bodies.

SWEETENER CLASSES: SUGAR ALCOHOLS, ARTIFICIAL, AND NATURAL

SUGAR ALCOHOLS: ERYTHRITOL, XYLITOL, MANNITOL, OTHER SWEETENERS THAT END IN -OL

Referring to sugar alcohols, Health Canada says, "a family of sweeteners also known as 'polyols' are used as food additives. They occur naturally in small amounts in fruits and vegetables, including berries, apples, and plums, but for large-scale commercial use they are manufactured from common sugars. While they are chemically very similar to sugars, they are less sweet than sugars and have fewer calories per gram."

In layman's terms, sugar alcohols are carbohydrates that are man-made from natural ingredients. The human body does not completely absorb these sugar alcohols. The tricky part is the word "completely."

In a basic keto nutrition equation, you subtract fibre from carbs to get your total net carbs. Sugar alcohols complicate this equation greatly. The keto world is split evenly between subtracting all the sugar alcohols from the equation and subtracting half to get the net carbs.

There is no definite rule for counting carbohydrate content in sugar alcohols; the effect differs for each individual. My suggestion is to be cautious whenever consuming food items that claim to be sugar- or carb-free. The very idea of "free" foods makes it easy to over consume. Overconsumption can result in digestive issues and in some cases weight gain. When you're on a low-carb or ketogenic diet, it's better to be safe than sorry and to always be skeptical. Always pay attention to any carbs consumed, even from sugar alcohols.

Note that sugar alcohols sometimes cause digestive distress, such as mild cramping or bloating.

Pure stevia contains no calories or carbs, and it has zero on the Glycemic Index. It has the added benefit of stabilizing blood sugar and insulin levels after a meal. Additionally, it is typically two to three hundred times sweeter than table sugar, meaning you only need to use a little to get a sweet taste in foods. Another benefit to using stevia is that it adds a slight nutrient boost.

ARTIFICIAL SWEETENERS: SACCHARIN, CYCLAMATE, ACESULFAME POTASSIUM, ASPARTAME, SUCRALOSE, ETC. (SWEET'N LOW, SPLENDA, EQUAL, ETC.)

Many of the most common artificial sweeteners found in processed and sugar-free foods, such as aspartame and sucralose, are advertised as low on the Glycemic index (GI) and low in calories, but we suggest using these with extreme caution or not at all. Part of the basis for the keto way of life is clean living, and you can't do that with a belly full of chemicals.

Artificial sweeteners are believed to be toxic to the brain; they destroy healthy gut bacteria and may even cause weight gain by deregulating metabolism. There is inconclusive evidence about the safety of these sweeteners over the long term.

Even though many of these sweeteners are listed as containing zero calories, be aware that legislation allows servings under 1 gram of carbohydrates and under 4 calories to be labelled as zero. So those little packets often pack a punch with about .999 grams of glucose/dextrose mixed with a small dose of an artificial sweetener to reach the desired sweetness.

We're crying foul on all artificial sweeteners. At the end of the day, they're just more chemicals that you and your body should avoid.

NATURAL SWEETENERS

These are naturally occurring sweeteners that are derived from plants, fruits, or vegetables. Some examples of natural sweeteners are stevia, erythritol, and monk fruit powder.

OUR RECOMMENDATIONS

Keep in mind that these are just that, our own recommendations. As always, we recommend that you practise due diligence and do your own research. Here's what we came up with, based on our own research and own experience.

THE GOOD

✓ **Stevia** [Natural sweetener | Sweetness: 200-350 times sweeter than sugar]

Stevia is extracted from the leaves of Stevia rebaudiana, a plant in the ragweed family. Stevia is commonly known as "sugar leaf" and has been safely used for thousands of years. South American tribes used stevia to sweeten tea and because it was believed to have healing properties.

 Consider purchasing a stevia plant from your local garden centre. You can grow your own sweetener, dry the leaves, and pulverize them with a mortar and pestle or a Magic Bullet. This guarantees you a clean source of sweet that you know you can trust.

Some people complain that stevia leaves a bitter aftertaste. This can be alleviated by adding a small pinch of pink salt.

Please note that certain brands of granulated stevia, such as Stevia in the Raw, can contain dextrose and/or maltodextrin.

✓ **Erythritol** [Sugar alcohol | Sweetness: 70% as sweet as sugar]

Erythritol was discovered in 1848 by Scottish chemist John Stenhouse and is derived from fruits, vegetables, and fermented foods. Erythritol is a carbohydrate that cannot be digested; it is quickly absorbed in the small intestine and is excreted through urine. Minimal amounts reach the colon; it causes very little gastric distress.

Erythritol has a Glycemic index of zero and has zero calories per gram. It is heat stable up to 160°C and is the most expensive of the sugar alcohols to produce, making it difficult for food manufacturers to use it in commercial products. Erythritol is not that sweet on its own, so it's often combined in foods and beverages with other sweeteners. It can have a slight "cooling" aftertaste, but when combined with other sweeteners, this is not very noticeable. Erythritol doesn't dissolve as easily as sugar, especially in the granulated format. We recommend grinding it in a Bullet or blender to reduce it to a confectioner's formula or powder.

Erythritol may not have any direct health benefits, but it has been proven to be noncarcinogenic, unlike many of the sweeteners that are not natural. It has also been shown to not feed bacteria in the mouth, so it is a good alternative to sugar in terms of dental health.

✓ **Monk fruit powder** [Natural sweetener | Sweetness: 300 times sweeter than sugar]

Monk fruit is a small melon-like fruit, also known as luo han guo or longevity fruit. It is named after the monks who originally harvested it in the southern mountains of China and in northern Thailand as early as the thirteenth century. It's three hundred times sweeter than sugar and has been used in traditional "Chinese medicine as a digestive aid and to treat obesity, diabetes, and the common cold."

Monk fruit has multiple medicinal benefits, including immune-boosting, anti-microbial, and antioxidant properties. It provides liver protection, helps to lower cholesterol, and also contains a compound that has the ability to inhibit tumour growth in pancreatic cancer. It does this by interfering with the rapid dividing of cancer cells and reducing blood flow to the tumour, promoting cancer cell death.

Monk fruit sweetener is made naturally from the juice of the fruit and provides a low-calorie sweetness without the insulin spikes of sugar. It's as sweet as stevia but without the bitter aftertaste of most stevia products.

✓ Swerve [Blended sweetener | Equivalent in sweetness to table sugar]

Swerve is an all-natural, no-calorie sweetener with excellent baking and cooking functionality. It is a short-chain carbohydrate that is derived from fruits and vegetables. It has the ability to brown and caramelize and is a great all-purpose substitute for sugar.

Swerve is a combination of erythritol, natural citrus flavour, and oligosaccharides, which are prebiotics, non-digestible food ingredients that stimulate the growth of prebiotic bacteria in the colon. We cannot digest and absorb oligosaccharides ourselves, as we lack the enzymes needed to break them down. Because of this, they don't affect blood sugar.

There are some health benefits associated with Swerve. Some studies show a reduction in cholesterol and triglycerides when using oligosaccharides. And of course, the prebiotics in the oligosaccharides help encourage beneficial gut bacteria.

THE BAD

✗ Xylitol [Sugar alcohol | Equivalent in sweetness to table sugar]

Xylitol is a sugar alcohol that naturally occurs in small amounts in the fibres of fruits and vegetables. It is produced commercially from corn cobs or birch trees. It's a sugar substitute that tastes like sugar but has fewer calories and is one of the most frequently used sweeteners in sugar-free chewing gum and mouthwash. Like erythritol, it's been shown to help with dental health by starving the bad bacteria in the mouth, thereby helping to prevent cavities. Xylitol can help to increase collagen production and may prevent osteoporosis. It's also used in cosmetics and medicines and may help promote good bacteria in the gut.

Xylitol has a Glycemic Index of 13, and only 50 percent is absorbed in your small intestine. It has minor impact on blood sugar and insulin levels when used in small amounts, but over 40 grams per day can cause gastric distress. Also, be aware that xylitol is very toxic for dogs, so if you have pets, choose another option.

✗ Maltitol [Sugar alcohol | 80 percent as sweet as sugar]

Maltitol is a sugar alcohol that is not a good choice for people on low-carb or ketogenic diets. It is the sweetener most often used in sugar-free candy, desserts, and other low-carb treats because it tastes similar to sugar and is considerably less expensive to produce than other sugar alcohols.

Maltitol has a high Glycemic Index (which means it spikes blood sugars) and can cause a lot of gastric distress. It is known for its laxative effects and is commonly associated with stomach issues including bloating, diarrhea, and abdominal pain. We recommend you avoid this one at all costs.

THE UGLY

✖ **Sucralose** [Artificial chemical sweetener | 320-1000 times sweeter than sugar]

Sucralose is a chemical sweetener that is produced by chlorinating sucrose. It is heavily debated in the keto world. Many claim it has a Glycemic Index of zero, while others say it drives their blood sugars through the roof.

There is a lack of evidence supporting the benefit of sucralose; in fact most data points to probable weight gain and the risk of heart disease with its use. Use of sucralose was rampant in the early 2000s, but with rumours of an unpublished study linking sucralose consumption with leukemia in rats, people began to shy away.

Chemical sweeteners such as sucralose have been shown to impact our primary immune systems by interrupting our gut bacteria. We recommend avoiding sucralose at all costs.

✖ **Aspartame** [Artificial chemical sweetener | 200 times sweeter than sugar]

Aspartame is a chemical sweetener made up of aspartic acid and phenylalanine. It is probably the most controversial sweetener of all. Numerous allegations have been made connecting aspartame to multiple sclerosis, systemic lupus, methanol toxicity, blindness, seizures, headaches, and mood changes.

Our recommendation is to avoid it, as there are many other safe and non-controversial sweeteners available. Better to be safe than sorry.

✖ **Saccharin** [Artificial chemical sweetener | 300-400 times sweeter than sugar]

Saccharin is a chemical sweetener manufactured by combining anthranilic acid, nitrous acid, sulfur dioxide, chlorine, and ammonia. (Yes, chlorine and ammonia!)

This is one of the oldest synthetic sweeteners, having made its first appearance around 150 years ago. After studies in the seventies linked saccharin use to cancer in rats, all saccharin products had to have a warning label explaining that it might induce cancer in people or animals. Saccharin is also known for leaving an extremely bitter aftertaste and has drastically decreased in commercial and personal use in recent times. We don't recommend the use of saccharin.

A FINAL WORD ON KETO SWEETENERS

While some sweeteners seem to be better than others, the best advice for ketogenic living, health, and weight loss is to learn to enjoy real foods in their unsweetened state. Although it might take a little time for you and your taste buds to adapt, you may discover a whole new appreciation for the natural, unprocessed flavour that is often masked by added sweeteners.

The jury is still out on whether some of these substitutes are truly harmless alternatives to sugar. Always exercise caution and research every label and every dish. Be careful what you eat. As always, moderation is key. It's unrealistic to think that we must go through life without indulging in a sweet treat, but in pursuit of health, be smart and choose wisely. The goal with the ketogenic diet is to remain in ketosis, so staying as close as possible to zero GI for sweeteners is the best choice.

KETO CONVERSIONS

Wondering how to convert these recipes back to non-keto? It's super easy. These conversions will help you out if you don't follow keto.

almond flour to regular flour is 1:1

coconut flour to regular flour is 1:3 or 1:4 (i.e., ¼ or ⅓ cup of coconut flour is equivalent to 1 cup regular flour)

note Coconut flour is much more absorbent that regular or almond flour. So you use less coconut flour and increase the number of eggs.

coconut sauce to soy sauce is 1:1

crème fraîche to sour cream is 1:1

crème fraîche to whipping cream is 1:¾ (i.e., 1 cup crème fraîche = ¾ cup 35% whipping cream)

erythritol: 1 tbsp + 1 tsp = 1 tbsp regular white sugar

fish sauce to Worcestershire sauce is 1:1

flax meal to regular flour is 1:2 (i.e., ½ cup flax meal = 1 cup flour)

flax seed to butter or oil is 3:1 (i.e., 3 tbsp flax seed = 1 tbsp butter or oil)

flax seed to egg: 1 tbsp flax seed + 3 tbsp water = 1 egg

liquid stevia: 6-9 drops = 1 tbsp regular white sugar

Swerve to regular white sugar is 1:1

xanthan gum to cornstarch is 1:1

APPENDIX D

TERMS TO KNOW

IN A KETOGENIC WORLD

ACV: apple cider vinegar

AS: artificial sweetener

BF: body fat

BG: blood glucose

BPC: bulletproof coffee

BP: blood pressure

BS: blood sugar

CICO: calories in, calories out (the now debunked idea that energy stored = energy in - energy out)

CKD: cyclical ketogenic diet (i.e., intaking large amounts of carbs one or two days a week to replenish glycogen stores; usually used in conjunction with extremely intense workouts)

CO: coconut oil

fat bomb: food item that is high in fat; used to help satisfy hunger

GI: Glycemic Index

gluconeogenesis: metabolic pathway that results in the generation of glucose from certain non-carbohydrate carbon substrates

glycolysis: the biochemical process of breaking down glucose into energy

HIIT: high-intensity interval training

HWC: heavy whipping cream, the American equivalent of 35% whipping cream

IF: intermittent fasting (a weight-loss tool where you fast in intervals; not recommended for beginners)

IIFYM: if it fits your macros

IR: insulin resistance

ketoacidosis: a metabolic state when the body cannot produce its own insulin and a high concentration of ketone bodies can lead to acidic blood levels (only happens in diabetics)

ketogenesis: the biochemical process of breaking down fatty acids into ketones

ketone: the alternate fuel your body will use when glucose is not available, typically through restriction of carbs

ketosis: a state that the body enters when there is no supply of carbohydrates for energy, our default metabolic state

LCHF: low carb, high fat (the basis of a ketogenic diet)

macros: macronutrients (i.e., fat, protein, and carbohydrates)

MCT: medium-chain triglycerides (fatty acids that bypass the usual digestive process and are instead transported directly to the liver to make ketones)

micros: micronutrients (i.e., the vitamins and minerals in our foods)

net carbs: calculation of the carbohydrates that are processed during digestion; calculated by subtracting the fibre and sugar alcohols from total carbohydrates

NSV: non-scale victory

NK: nutritional ketosis (achieved by restricting carbs)

OMAD: one meal a day (a version of intermittent fasting whereby one attempts to fit daily macros into one meal)

SAD: standard American diet

SF: sugar-free

T1D: type 1 diabetes

T2D: type 2 diabetes

woosh: after a stall, a substantial overnight weight loss

WOE: way of eating

WOL: way of life